Rapture

Rapture

An Anthology of Performance Poetry from Aotearoa New Zealand

Edited by **Carrie Rudzinski** and **Grace Iwashita-Taylor**
with a foreword by **Chris Tse**

AUCKLAND UNIVERSITY PRESS

First published 2023
Auckland University Press
University of Auckland
Private Bag 92019
Auckland 1142
New Zealand
www.aucklanduniversitypress.co.nz

ISBN 978 1 86940 980 7

Published with the assistance of Creative New Zealand

creative nz
ARTS COUNCIL OF NEW ZEALAND TOI AOTEAROA

A catalogue record for this book is available from the
National Library of New Zealand

Design and cover image by Seven.co.nz

This book was printed on FSC® certified paper

Printed in China by Everbest Printing Investment Ltd

Contents

Foreword

I knew I shouldn't read the comments, but sometimes curiosity gets the better of me (plus, as a Libra, I can't help but crave a little validation). I'd been given the opportunity to perform a poem on television and I thought that reading the comments on the accompanying Facebook post about my appearance might give me some insight into what the general public thinks about poetry. What I saw wasn't negative or mean per se, but one innocuous comment stood out and stuck with me: 'More of a story than a poem.' I'm not sure why this particular piece of feedback ran laps around my brain for the next few weeks – I would swing between vehemently disagreeing with it and questioning whether my poems were actually poems (not a great frame of mind for someone who has just been appointed New Zealand Poet Laureate). The more I thought about this casual dismissal of my poem, the more I began to question my creative practice as a poet: What makes a poem a poem, and who even gets to define what poetry is? I kept asking myself: Well, why can't poems be like stories? After all, poetry began as an oral tradition, a way to pass on folklore, history, genealogy and the law before the advent of the written word. In an Aotearoa context, Māori and Pasifika oral tradition predates contact with Pākehā and their written literary forms. Human beings are hardwired to use storytelling to understand the world around us and to share information with others – poetry is just one of the many tools we have in our narrative toolbox. It can be many things – it's an ever-shifting creature, shedding skins and borrowing qualities from other literary genres and forms.

It was hearing poetry performed live that made me want to take being a poet more seriously. Although I'd studied the ins and outs of poetry at school and had taken to writing poems to share with my friends during lunch breaks, it wasn't until I started attending open mics and other spoken-word events that I realised there's more to poetry than what was enshrined on the page or taught by my teachers. One of the first events I attended in the early 2000s while studying English literature and creative writing at university was the regular Poets Pub open mic at the Angus Inn in Lower Hutt. That's where I took the leap from being a bedroom poet to an open mic poet and started to share my work with an audience of mostly strangers (I'd drag my best friends along for moral support, and even convinced them to read on occasion). It was a somewhat chaotic place to perform – the MC had the extroverted personality of a television show presenter on speed, and I distinctly remember having to compete with the sing-song pokie machines and the clattering of glasses being loaded into the dishwasher behind the bar. Some of the regulars were only there for a quiet pint and couldn't care less about the poetry. And yet there was something thrilling about this chaos – it was so removed from sitting in a classroom or lecture theatre analysing poetry and treating it as static, sacred text. It was also where I first heard poems about queer love and mental health, a far cry from what I'd been prescribed at school. These topics may seem mainstream to today's younger poets and readers, who have been exposed to a much wider range of poets and poetry from a young age, but for me it was somewhat outré, and I wouldn't appreciate how meaningful this was to me until much later. The Poets Pub was where I learned that poetry can have a very different life beyond what most of us see on the page, where a charged performance of a poem can bring audiences to tears and/or rapturous applause.

As the editors of *Rapture* note in their introduction, open mic nights and regular spoken-word events are the cornerstones of local poetry communities throughout Aotearoa, giving poets of all calibres and backgrounds the opportunity to share their work in supportive environments. Even when the stakes are high at a poetry slam, you can guarantee that the audience is backing each and every single poet to succeed. These events also attract a noticeable abundance of poets from marginalised communities, many of whom have been shut out of, or are wary of, traditional literary and publishing platforms. These poets utilise the spoken-word form and its many variations to claim a space for themselves and to tackle the often complicated issues that affect their communities. It's no wonder then, that spoken word continues to be an attractive creative outlet for young people to draw attention to, and participate in conversations about, issues such as climate change, LGBTQIA+ rights and equality. In a world where young people's futures and wellbeing are at stake and being systematically eroded by those in power, having a voice and being able to utilise it, including through poetry, cannot be undervalued. Dr Lucy English, a Professor of Creative Enterprise and The Spoken Word at Bath Spa University, wrote in 2016: 'Aside from the obvious entertainment spin that spoken word puts on this traditional form of literature, it's now being (rightly) recognised for its positive impact on the mental wellbeing of performers.'[1] Last year, I spoke with Travis Cottreau for a magazine article about Wellington's spoken-word scene. In his capacity as producer and MC of the long-running Poetry in Motion series, he's seen first-hand how new poets have taken to spoken word as a way to help them work through their personal struggles with mental health, gender identity, sexuality and trauma. For some of these poets, spoken word was more than just about expression or catharsis – it was a lifeline.

Poetry has been that lifeline for me at various points in my life, and while I write mostly for the page, there's no denying that getting to perform my work has played an important part in my growth as a poet and as a person. I've had the opportunity and privilege of performing in both traditional and unconventional settings – there have been readings at bookstores, libraries, galleries and bars, as well as marae, boardrooms, gay saunas and shipping containers. As a member of the Show Ponies, I've collaborated with dancers and choreographers, and in the United Kingdom I performed with Tongue Fu, a collective that improvises soundtracks while poets perform their work. These experiences rank as some of my most memorable as a poet, and they've helped me to reach audiences

1 'The Growing Popularity of Performance Poetry is a Boost for Mental Wellbeing', *Guardian*, 2 June 2016, www.theguardian.com/culture-professionals-network/2016/jun/02/performance-poetry-boost-for-mental-wellbeing

who might otherwise never have come across my work or who prefer to engage with poetry via performance rather than on the page. For me, this reinforces the fact that we are drawn to stories being told to us, and while encountering a poem on the page does have its advantages (time to process and revisit), the transformation that takes place through performance stirs something within all of us.

Rapture presents a parallel narrative about contemporary Aotearoa poetry – one that isn't anchored in the pages of literary journals or (until now) on bookshop shelves. This timely and expansive anthology brings together a dynamic range of voices, from poets with award-winning collections to slam champions and theatre makers. There's crossover and cross-pollination with 'traditional' or 'page' poetry, and a desire to dissolve the arbitrary borders set up by the supposed 'page versus stage' binary. While both camps of poetry have their own qualities or quirks, they share a common goal – to communicate and connect through words and storytelling. Those who may be sceptical of spoken-word and performance poetry may be surprised at the broad range of voices, styles and forms on display in this collection. The editors of *Rapture* aren't preoccupied with asking what poetry *is* – instead, the question is: What does poetry *do*? The words contained herein are designed to make us feel something, to change minds and hearts, and to move and inspire those who may read or hear these words. These poems are stories, and much more. Whether you're meeting the poets in this collection on the page for the first time or have had the fortune of seeing them perform in the flesh, this anthology reminds us all that the relationship between 'page' and 'stage' poetry isn't *or*, it's *and*.

Chris Tse
New Zealand Poet Laureate 2022–2024
April 2023

Introduction

We acknowledge mana whenua, the indigenous people who have historic and territorial rights over the land and sea of Aotearoa. We pay respect to all ancestors – past, present and future – and acknowledge that we, as editors, are tauiwi in Aotearoa New Zealand.

These poems riot in harmony.

These poems roam the streets looking for a fight, question who we are and who we are growing into, examine the weaponisation and reclaiming of language. These poems take lovers to bed, scream into the depths of sadness and reclaim bodies. These poems decolonise and re-indigenise, swim in the moana, reshape the word 'home'. These poems belly laugh deep, sprawl out under a blanket of stars and point into the wonder, wax nostalgic for the friends we have and the friends we have lost. These poems are family – a brilliant representation of the diversity of voice, talent, experience and desires of real writers, real poets, real people of Aotearoa.

Rapture is a snapshot of performance poetry in Aotearoa New Zealand over the past decade, aiming to reveal and celebrate the diverse voices of performance poets, rappers, spoken-word artists, slam poets, theatre makers, genre blenders and storytellers.

For decades, performance poetry has been cast to the fringes of academia and literature with some people questioning the legitimacy and craftsmanship of writers who read their work out loud with passion and expertise. Some like to say there are 'page poets' and there are 'stage poets'. But there are countless people, initiatives and platforms that have worked to combat this narrative and who have contributed to the elevation of performance poetry's recognition as a legitimate literary art form in Aotearoa. Legendary poets like Sam Hunt, Tusiata Avia and Selina Tusitala Marsh launched poetry out of the pages of books and into rock concerts, off-Broadway theatres and the halls of Westminster Abbey. Secondary school teachers and university lecturers have used spoken-word artists' recordings within their curriculum as a dynamic way to engage students who may otherwise feel disconnected from literature. And countless writers have stepped up to microphones on stages – from TEDx to WOMAD to renowned literary festivals – and opened their mouths to thunderous applause.

We hope this anthology inspires academics, publishers, literary giants and funding bodies to lift our voices with the same passion audiences have embraced us with. This collection of poems is only a small sample of the immense talent in Aotearoa and it is our sincere hope that it sparks our poetry community to create future collections.

Contributions to *Rapture* are from an open submission call for performance poetry from poets who have a connection with Aotearoa. We were overwhelmed by the response, with over 600 poems submitted and the knowledge that so many more could have been collected. We selected poems that spoke to us as readers, audience members and fellow poets. We wanted to be moved, to feel vulnerability, to have our world view shifted, and each of these poems delivered. These poems sing, rage, celebrate and reflect the world we exist in. They challenge and confront us, pushing readers to grow and reconsider what they know and understand.

Performance poems are often personal and political but this collection of work is also imaginative, visceral and vibrant. It is this realness that has built a mighty wave of talent that is thriving and reinvigorating poetry to audiences in Aotearoa today. Let's not forget that reading solitarily is a relatively new phenomenon. Poets have been revered as oral storytellers throughout history, often calling out injustices as they happen.

This craft requires immense skill: not only do writers utilise poetic devices, word play, editing and literary skills but poets bring their work to life with physical and vocal performances. Bringing words to life with intonation, honesty and strength is a special talent and puts performing poetry in a blended genre between the literary and theatrical. This anthology is a reclamation: performance poetry has shaped and saved the lives of many artists and their audiences. It is also a declaration: we are not going anywhere.

The lifeline and joy of an art form is discovering new voices: those who change the landscape with their unique perspective or push the boundaries of what was thought possible. The way young people have connected with spoken word in Aotearoa is electric – it is an entry point for them to access literature and an activation of ownership over their own voices. Anyone can step in front of the mic and ignite a crowd with their own story. Youth poets are engaged and committed to developing their craft, using their art to fight systemic injustices and give hope to those listening. We are grateful for the emerging voices represented in this collection and we look forward to those who will continue to shape the path forward.

Performance poetry is alive today in schools, universities, writers festivals, fringe festivals, theatre stages, pubs, libraries, street corners and on the page. The landscape of the poetry community in Aotearoa is anchored deeply by the opportunity to cultivate spaces for writers to share their words and worlds. We acknowledge the following initiatives as significant parts of the tapestry that make up our poetry community: Poetry Live | Poetry Idol | Rising Voices Youth Poetry Movement | South Auckland Poets Collective | Catalyst | Printable Reality | NZ National Poetry Slam | Inside Out Open Mic Night | Poetry in Motion | JAFA Poetry Slam | Motif Poetry Ruri Tūtohu | Action Education | WORD – The Front Line | Auckland Writers Festival | WORD Christchurch | Verb Wellington | Nelson, Māpua and Golden Bay Live Poets | New Zealand Young Writers Festival | Blackmail Press | The Literatti | Tagata Pasifika Resources & Development Trust | Street Poets Black | Going West Poetry Festival and Slam | WOMAD | Stand Up Poetry | and so many more, with none greater than the other.

Behind every open mic night, poetry slam and poetry initiative are people and the time dedicated, often in a voluntary capacity, to cultivate and hold space so that poets and poetry have a home. We celebrate every event organiser, teaching artist, mentor, producer, collective, poetry development programme leader – past, present and future – who has given their time, energy and expertise to provide these spaces for our community.

Many poets have carved a space within theatre, blending genres and definitions of what poetry can do and where it can exist. Theatre provides the opportunity for world building beyond just the voice, utilising the dynamics of lighting, staging, costume, sound design and performance to complement the written word. Of notable mention, some poetic theatre works over the last fifteen years include *Wild Dogs Under My Skirt* and *The Savage Coloniser Show* (Tusiata Avia), *My Own Darling* (Grace Iwashita-Taylor), *Scenes from a Yellow Peril* (Nathan Joe), *How We Survive* and *Hysterical* (Carrie Rudzinski and Olivia Hall), *Show Ponies* (Freya Daly Sadgrove), *Chrome Dome* and *Schizo* (Dan Goodwin), *Jagged Little Pilgrimage* (Ali Jacs), *45 Cents an Hour* and *Your Heart Looks Like a Vagina* (Dominic Hoey) and *UPU* (curated by Grace Iwashita-Taylor, directed by Fasitua Amosa).

We love that this collection is not bound by a theme or a topic. In Mohamed Hassan's powerful poem '(Un)learning My Name' we are introduced to a central thread found in many of the poems in this collection: the reclaiming of identity, culture and language – of self. Other poems in these pages will surprise with their imagery and imagination, unpacking a simple moment like Laura Borrowdale's 'Guilt', which opens with the admission 'I am a bad mother', or their ability to expertly navigate themes of womanhood, reclamation and decolonisation as in Stevie Davis-Tana's 'Te Awa Atua'.

While performance poets are sometimes referred to as spoken-word artists or slam poets, it's important to note that 'poetry slams' are a specific competition in which poets participate. They are a game for our art form where we ask random members of the audience to assign numbers to our work to take our egos down a few notches. Slams are a special way to build community and you'll find many taking place in cities, regions and schools across Aotearoa, with several culminating in well-known platforms like the NZ National Poetry Slam finals, WORD – The Front Line and Poetry Idol.

At poetry slams, each competition begins with a sacrificial poem – an offering to warm up the audience and whet the palates of the judges – in preparation for the show that will follow. And so, as editors, we offer ourselves as sacrificial poets, to humbly set the stage for the incredible selection of work that represents our community, our whānau, our country.

Andy Coyle then welcomes you with his poem 'I fell in love at the poetry night', which frames the environment and energy at an open mic night. In the collection that follows, each poet will step onto the page and introduce themselves before speaking life into their poem. In these performances you'll discover fresh new voices interwoven with internationally renowned legends of our scene.

Rapture is split into three sections: poems that make us want to burn down injustice and scream into the wild; poems that suspend us in time and heal as we float in the rains that come after the fires; and poems that ground our roots in the earth as we learn to grow again.

Thank you for picking up this anthology, a collection that provides a snapshot of the dynamic fluidity of our performance-poetry community. We invite you to lean in, soak up the words, click, snap, holla and engage with these voices, these stories, these truth-tellers.

Carrie Rudzinski and Grace Iwashita-Taylor

RISING VOICES, LET ME HEAR YOUR STORIES, THE BONES AND SKIN OF IT, THE GRIT AND BITE OF IT, THE TRUTH OF ALL OF IT, RISING VOICES.

— Jai MacDonald & Grace Iwashita-Taylor,
Rising Voices Youth Poetry Movement

Carrie Rudzinski (she/her) has performed her work over the past seventeen years across six countries and has been featured in *Bustle, HuffPost* and *Teen Vogue*. She ranked fourth in the world at the 2014 Womxn of the World Poetry Slam and co-founded Auckland's JAFA Poetry Slam. Her poems have been published in *Landfall, The Spinoff, Stasis, Catalyst* and *Muzzle*. Carrie is the co-creator of two poetry theatre shows – *How We Survive* (2019) and *Hysterical* (2022), the latter of which won Best New Play at the Wellington Theatre Awards and Outstanding Performance Poetry at the Auckland Fringe Festival.

Always A Godmother / Never A God

When I talk to my mother
on the phone
she is 18 hours
behind me in time:

my life came from her
life and I live in her future

I am her laugh
exploding out
an open window
into God's hungry mouth

My mother has always believed
in God and I have always believed
in her:

she is more prayer
than person / her voice
the only sound
in this world
I crave

and I ask her
if God learned everything he knows
from his mother too?

My mother carved me from her ribs
a soft weapon made of bone

My body skin of spoiled milk
freckled lips and hips
My short shorts and shaved head

My mother / the god who made me
says I cannot go anywhere without
stealing the eyeballs of humans
who do not deserve the honour
of looking at me

And we laugh / we women
as tall as redwoods
no pierced ears
or lipstick
to hide us

and I ask her
if every human on this planet
came from inside a woman
why would we ever believe
God was a man?

But we both know
no God Mother would allow
this world to exist

so like all mothers before her
she's taught me how to live
in a world full of men

My mother tells me
that when she was at university
there was a series of campus rapes
and when walking home at night
she would wear a men's jacket
and raise the hood
so she might be mistaken
for a man

so she might survive
what it is to be a woman

and I ask her if one woman survives
does another cry out in the dark?

Once / I stood on a street corner
in Denver / Delhi / Detroit
and a man licked the length
of my legs with his eyeballs

Once / a man asked me to smile
and when I didn't / he called me
a cunt

Once / I discovered there is no record
for the maiden names of my great-
grandmothers and whole women
went up in smoke

Once / they called me Sir
as if my body had not been forced
to beg for survival while walking
through a city

My body the machete
My body the miracle
my mother gave me
My body praying to some unseen god
but my mother was the only one
to ever pray back

My mother the moon I howl to
in the dark

she taught me to slit their throats
with my tongue
to rip out their teeth
and remind them
of the ghost women
I come from

but I am always a Godmother
never a god

so like all the women before me
who birthed a man
only to have him strangle their daughters
in the dark

I pray to myself

I pick up the phone
and wait for my mother's voice

like the ocean waits
to lift my body
in a wave

like a man waits
to watch me
cross the street

like a Godmother
waits to give birth
to a new god.

Grace Iwashita-Taylor, breathing bloodlines from Samoa, England and Japan, is an artist of upu dedicated to carving, elevating and holding spaces for storytellers of Te Moana-nui-a-Kiwa. She was awarded the Creative New Zealand Arts Pasifika Emerging Artist in 2014 and the Auckland Mayoral Writers Grant in 2016. Her achievements include holding the visiting international writer in residence at the University of Hawai'i in 2018, and co-founding Rising Voices Youth Poetry Slam and the South Auckland Poets Collective. Grace wrote *My Own Darling* (2015), co-created and curated *UPU* (2020), co-directs Flying Fetu and the Flying Fetu Festival, and has published two poetry collections, *Afakasi Speaks* (2013) and *Full Broken Bloom* (2017), with Ala Press.

Lagimalie | balance for the heavens in you

in the spiral
there exists the locked jaw
            grind
the womxn with no words
but her entire body speaking
so tense so tense so tense
even her bones hurt
            grind
            halt
            grind
            speak now
            answer now
the pain she absorbed and the pain expelling
all at once   always all at once
cellular memory exposed
no elders to massage her
flickers of coloured lights
trick her vision
she can only now imagine
they are ancestors
she silently tries to find her breath
find her breath find her breath find her breath find her breath

this usually takes 3 days
and when it is done
another skin
discarded

inhale
tasi
lua
tolu
fa

hold
tasi
lua

exhale
ono
lima
fa
tolu
lua
tasi

expand the canal
always with water
salty
and hot
heated by the breath of your ancestors
that is how deep the utu has been buried

lift up the bones
ask them their story
fish for the fihi / entanglement
tend to the sala / mala / harm
seek to vevete / unbind it
find the estranged weave in the fala
honour the decay
then clean the bones

do not do this alone

intergenerational healing
starts with you, but
it is a communal task

you were birthed from the blue amniotic fluid
of an ancestor that is present, contemporary
unbound by tā / time

you are the vā

do not grieve for the ancestors you have not yet met
their DNA is within you
your atoms and cells match and house the residue of them

you are the ancestor you have been waiting for

so heal your own trauma in the present
and by default
this heals the trauma of them
and your children
breaking the cycle

suffering is not a virtue

be the vā
that reinstates a state of noa to your gafa
restore lagimalie
harmony
balance

this is our birthright

inhale
    tasi
    lua
    tolu
    fa

hold
    tasi
    lua

exhale
    ono
    lima
    fa
    tolu
    lua
    tasi

THE POINT IS NOT THE POINTS. THE POINT IS THE PEOPLE.

— Ken Arkind

Andy Coyle's first collection, *Ode to the Cyclist and Other Poems*, was published in 2015 by the Republic of Oma Rāpeti Press. He has represented Christchurch twice in the NZ National Poetry Slam finals, and appeared at WORD Christchurch, the Wellington Jazz Festival, the Newtown Festival, LitCrawl, the Street Party in the Lyttelton Harbour Festival of Lights, Gap Filler and Fringe festivals in Auckland, Wellington and Dunedin. In 2017–2018 Andy curated a poetry performance series at the infamous Hell Fire Club in Lyttelton and released an award-winning anthology documenting that series. Andy lives in Lyttelton.

This poem was first published in *Ode to the Cyclist and Other Poems*.

I fell in love at the poetry night

dedicated to Doc Drumheller and Ciaran Fox on the tenth anniversary of the Catalyst Poetry Open Mic night

I fell in love at the poetry night with poets,
dozens of them,
mumblers, mutterers, majestic moonlighters,
stumblers, stutterers, out-of-work freedom fighters,
rebels with or without a cause,
capable of hijacking your heart in every pause,
chauvinists, feminists, masochists
self-obsessed hypocrites,
addicts, fanatics, hopeless romantics,
each archetype immersed in their own
private world of semantics.

I fell in love at the poetry night
with the meter of the verse,
steady rhythms and free-flowing rhyme,
visionary prophets gliding on intuitive time,
the hopeful expression of these beautiful minds,
dropping line after line of pure crystal myths.
Getting high on communication,
carefully crafted or
stream of consciousness never redrafted,
ranters and whisperers
screamers and dreamers
exploring the loftiest themes with the best intentions,
or unravelling the intricate fabric of their own depression,
I'm with you for every word, every session.

I fell in love at the poetry night
with crazy girls who know how to cause a scene,
who say who they are and say what they mean.

I fell in love with shy girls who like to watch,
who keep their poems hidden in journals under pillows
for one day granddaughters to discover at last
and wonder at how their dear old nana had such a
passionate past.

I fell in love with exhibitionists
who just have to get it out there
all of it, anytime, anywhere.

I fell in love with poetic comedy
lulling us into a false sense of security
then whipping the rug out from beneath us
using an orator's skill to turn a room
in and out of moods at will.

I fell in love with the masters of restraint,
    painting their poems over an audience
with layer upon layer of latent imagery.

I fell in love with the hard-earned
    poetry of the street,
tumbling fast and proud from eloquent mouths
like scrambling children's feet down
a wooden school corridor
where similes drift off to sleep
and metaphors silently weep
knowing that their definitions are already forgotten.

I fell in love with conscious political incisions,
challenging us to re-evaluate our visions
and to set our rambling paths onto
higher missions.

I even fell in love on the way to the poetry night
with a madman on the bus
who whispered his poems uninvited through
yellow teeth,
rocking, chanting
real-life poems
conducting real-life pain in simple tortured
memorised refrains.

I fell in love at the poetry night
with poets, dozens of them,
be they the rolling thunder type blunderers
who just wanna get their energies heard

or be they the meticulous revisionary types
who believe with impenitent devotion
in the economy of words,

all poets are on a mystical path
through the transitional nature of language,

through incantation and ceremony
we invite another being through a doorway,
a deliberate channel
or an accidental shaman,
the act of transcendence
through intuitive recitation,
the art of interpreting signs
the receivers of voices
the secret practitioners of ancient traditions.

I fell in love at the poetry night
with poets,
dozens of them.

1

Burn it down

Tusiata Avia is an internationally acclaimed poet, writer and performer. She has published four collections of poetry and four children's books. Based on her debut poetry collection of the same name, *Wild Dogs Under My Skirt* (2019) showed Off-Broadway in 2020 and won the Fringe Encore Series Outstanding Production of the Year. Tusiata was appointed a Member of the New Zealand Order of Merit for services to poetry and the arts in 2020 and her most recent collection, *The Savage Coloniser Book* (Victoria University Press, 2020), won the Mary and Peter Biggs Award for Poetry at the 2021 Ockham New Zealand Book Awards. Her new play based on that book premiered in 2023.

This poem was first published in *Fale Aitu | Spirit House* (Victoria University Press, 2016).

Apology

My body is not an apology
not a hiding place
not an arranged and artful fortress

my body is not a vapid pool of water
my body is not draped
it is not imagined into another shape or texture

not to you, Beloved
my body is a waterfall of flesh
my body is a herd of animals, fat and groaning for the bliss of slaughter

it is the celebration running down the faces of the famished
it is handfuls and handfuls
it is marrow and jelly and sizzling fat dripping steadily into the bonfire

my body is a baptism, a confessional
my body is the vows of a hundred thousand virgin soldiers
my body is the war that scours the earth

my body is the shalom and the salaam
my body is the mother shot suddenly in the street
my body is the mother dying slowly

my body is the frightened child coaxed out from beneath the body
of her fallen mother with a promise of honey
my body is the honey drowning the blind, the halt, the deaf, the mute

my body is the hospital
my body is the orphanage
my body is a hundred ice creams lined up like parents

my body is the alofa and the aroha
my body is the Sinai, the Red Sea, Hawai'i
my body is a room full of ancestors hurtling through the hole in my chest

Hine-nui-te-pō, Pelé, Nafanua, Isis, Aphrodite
their arms and legs and hair, hot and wet and tangled as they leave
my body is the distance between our bones, Beloved

my body loses its mind and its manners
my body is quivering, slippery, flushed as a newborn
my body is your mother

my body is your medicine
my body is the midwife hastening your own birth
pulling you out from inside the womb of your self

my body is the Qur'an, the Torah
my body is the Christ
my body is the prophetess, the Samoan goddess of war

my body leaves the underworld and rows across the oceans
my body is wet from the journey and frightens those who run to meet me
my body knows only of itself

which is the whole world
and the sky and the moon
and the planets spinning

my body catches them all in a net made of skin
my body is the tent of my body
and dwells here on earth among us.

**First line is credited to Sonya Renee Taylor*

Mohamed Hassan is an award-winning writer and journalist from Auckland and Cairo. He was the 2015 NZ National Poetry Slam champion and placed second at the 2021 UK National Poetry Slam. He has toured his work across New Zealand, Australia, the US and UK, and his poems are taught in hundreds of schools internationally. His first poetry collection, *National Anthem* (Dead Bird Books, 2020), was shortlisted for the 2021 Ockham New Zealand Book Awards, and his bestselling essay collection, *How to Be a Bad Muslim*, was published in 2022 by Penguin Random House.

This poem was first published in *National Anthem*.

(Un)Learning My Name

/Mohamed/
/Moh.ham.ed/
/Mo....................haaaam.................ed/

The first time I am mistaken
for a white man I feel a rush
of joy / lurching from my gut
/ a relief

I have finally won a place
a right to invisibility
/ a belong

if only for a moment

a wicked pleasure that I have fit
so well in today / a passing thought
a comma on a blank page
/ it doesn't last

I am asked what my name is
and I flinch / the jig is up
I am caught in a
/ lie

/Moh.ham.ed/

The familiarity fades
a little flicker once lit
behind the eyes isn't
for me anymore

/ the third stage of grief
is bargaining

but you look so much like us *you don't*
look Arab at all
where do you get your blue eyes from *they are so beautiful*
it must be somewhere in your bloodline *we*
must be
this beautiful *which parts of your ancestry*
do you owe us *which parts*
have you stolen

/Moh.ham.ed/

I have spent my life
carving vowels
out of my throat
so my name will be

/ easier to say

sanding down
my grandfather
so I could fit him in
a carry-on bag
a driver's licence
a job interview

/Moh-ham-ed/
adjective: *praised one;*
thanked in the earth and sky;

I am pouring oil down my throat
until it lines my stomach
until no guttural could ever

/ escape

I still say it the way my first
white teacher said it
the way she corrected me
in front of the class
until I learnt how to stumble

/ over
/ my identity
/ the way
/ she did

How to strip away
parts of myself
that couldn't be marketed
to a Western

/ tongue

I still shave off my curly
hair and wear blue
to bring out my eyes

so beautiful!
where did they?

/Muh.ha.med/
/Moحa.mad/
/حمam.mad/

It takes me nineteen years

to learn / how to pronounce
my own name

/ in public

The first time I say it
the way my mother
did when she named me

/محمد/

It feels like I have

/ stolen
something back.

Nafanua Purcell Kersel claims lineage from the villages of Falealupo-tai, Mosula, Malaela, Satufia and Tuaefu in Samoa. Raised in Te Whanganui-a-Tara, she now lives in Te Matau-a-Māui with her husband and three children. Her first experience of sharing poetry was through Poetry with Brownies and she is the 2020 Hawke's Bay Poetry Slam champion. Nafanua is a recent graduate of the International Institute of Modern Letters at Te Herenga Waka Victoria University of Wellington and her poetry has been published in *Vā: Stories by Women of the Moana* (Tatou Publishing, 2021), *Vines* and *Turbine | Kapohau.*

This poem was first published in literary arts journal *Vines* 3 (2021).

Names 'n' Shit

Even before you know *all* of my names
you ask me to teach you
how to say 'shit' in Samoan
so you can, what?
offend me in my own language?
stick *my* mother tongue out at parties?
just for laughs, eh?   ha   ha

before this, I would have given you the story of my name
defined-in-full
would have told you that its first carrier was
goddess-come-warrior, diplomat-come-prophetess
but you won't know that now because
you   never   asked

so I ask myself – shall I surrender that one 'shitty' syllable?
for you to spit and slap into submission
coin, the term –
deposit, its rich –
claim, reward points
for your
brown-card clout chasing ass?

hmmm. Yes.
in the spirit of my Great Name, I will teach you
that the word for shit
is how we say *your* name in Samoan.
Just for laughs, eh? Ha-ha.

For My Wairua (she/her) is atua anointed and wairua driven, based on the notion that creating heals and healing creates. For My Wairua is resistance against the dominant discourse and is proof that if you have blood in your veins and tīpuna in your thoughts, you can create. With reclamation at the core, For My Wairua seeks to navigate the vast oceans of life as a fat, indigenous Māori and Pasifika wahine. For My Wairua is in its infancy, writing mainly for Instagram audiences and working as a self-published author on Substack.

Stereotypical Māori

The captivating Māori
The waiata Māori
The Louis Vuitton Māori

The 'smart for a' Māori
The mean Māori (mean)
The *Police 10/7* Māori

The 'don't speak te reo' Māori
The 'never grew up on the marae' Māori
The 'who do you come from' Māori

The blood quantum Māori
The 1/4 Māori
The sign along the dotted line Māori
The uprising of Māori
The resilience of Māori
The brilliance of Māori

Nathan Joe (he/him) is a Chinese Kiwi playwright and performance poet, originally from Ōtautahi. He is the 2020 NZ National Poetry Slam champion and 2021 Bruce Mason Playwriting Award winner. In 2022, Nathan released poetry short film *Homecoming Poems* and performed in his play *Scenes from a Yellow Peril*, which premiered at the ASB Waterfront Theatre. He is the creator behind BIPOC spoken-word line up *Dirty Passports* (2021) and theatrical experiment *Gay Death Stocktake* (2022). Nathan's other performance highlights include TEDx Auckland and Freya Daly Sadgrove's *Show Ponies.*

MY ANCESTORS CROSSED OCEANS TO BE HERE AND ALL I HAVE TO SHOW FOR IT IS THIS BUBBLE TEA

In the wreckage of my culture
In the wreckage of my mother leaving motherland
When the ships came to shore
And smashed against the rocks

Leaving

Language
Art   great literature

Ancestral homes

And lineage far behind them

All that remains in me
Is a name I no longer use

                    A name twisted unfamiliar

All that remains are
Memes of self-mockery

                    Look at how my parents have traumatised me

LOL

Look at how bad my Chinese is

LOL

Look at how bad I am at math

LOL

anime   LOL

model minority   LOL

K-pop   LOL

and I lolled and I lolled and I lolled

and I can barely hear myself thinking (over the sound of this lolling laughter)
this rolling yellow wave tumbling (yellow white river rippling)
self-deprecation turned self-decapitation

I can barely hear my   self
Self-hood   self-harmed
Over the loud sipping of   bubble tea
Korean bbq   or   potluck
The clipping of buy 9 cups and get one free
I can barely remember The Treaty

Amongst
this ocean of white noise rippling
replicated   and   highlighted   made
Yellow
Yellow
Yellow

It's a strange paradox to leave something behind and also to wish to keep it with you.
Is that hypocrisy or just human nature?

It's a strange paradox to live in a body that does not feel like yours

White people call it dissociation
I just call it being Asian

Is it problematic to say colonised cultures have the privilege

No   do not call it   privilege

But is it wrong to say colonised cultures
have more culture to pass down
because they have fought for their survival?

They are fighting for their survival

Fight or flight
Do or die

(my toothless bite suckles on your Pākehā teet)

The traveller

The immigrant

The diaspora

Dispersing

Who left willingly

Dispersing

Who consented to
Some degree
Of his or her own
Annihilation

Dispersing

And dispersed of their own doing

The question isn't
Where are you from?

But why did you come here?

Why did you come knowing what you would lose?

What were you running from?

And where will you go
when there is nowhere
left to go?

Dominic Hoey is a poet, author and playwright based in Auckland. His debut novel *Iceland* (Steele Roberts, 2017) was a New Zealand bestseller, long-listed for the 2018 Ockham New Zealand Book Awards, and his short story '1986' won the 2021 Sunday Star-Times Short Story Award. Dominic has written and performed two one-person hit shows about his bone disease and his inability to get arts funding. In a former life, Dominic was an MC battle and slam-poetry champion. His latest novel, *Poor People with Money* (Penguin Random House, 2022), spent nine weeks on the New Zealand bestseller list and received rave reviews. Currently he lives with a small, vicious dog and dreams of one day owning an animal rescue farm.

stories

all my life i wanted to tell you stories
about the time we was in love drunk driving through the streets
the city shimming beneath us
about our friends and the pain written over their beautiful bodies
about feeling so numb, some days i didn't flinch when you cut me

i wanted to tell you about special education
an ironic name since the only thing we learnt in that tiny classroom was that we was worthless
about the ghosts in the walls whispering of lost summers
and how i found drugs and turned hollywood; indestructible and dumb

i wanted to tell you about falling in love so hard i woke up concussed
about standing on stage that first time
vomit on my shoes, my skin no longer see through
about the shame-filled midnights
both of us fools
running headlong into burning bridges

i wanted to tell you about how this city's not made of concrete
a mosaic of broken people
co-existing among the rats and the pigeons and the rich
about the red-light jesus
throwing filthy holy water over teslas
telling me
'you can't beg for change you gotta take it'
about the night my reflection stepped from a shop window walked towards me
and i thought of how time makes clichés of us all

i wanted to tell you about sitting in an empty bar
us talking gentle bullshit until our beers turned to sand
about how we only ever speak of houses and never homes
and if i had a dollar for every landlord
who stole my sleep
we'd be able to afford to rent here
but nah
no artists in rugby city
where they paint the town shit green
strip mine the night
until strip malls line the curb

i wanted to tell you about walking an endless dawn
standing together atop an apartment building
rusting empty against the skyline
looking out at the spiderweb that stretches to the city limits
out there
beneath the security light moon
where all is right in the world
of fast food ideologies and perfect debt
i wanted to tell you all of this
all of it
so you would remember
and make it real

Eliana Gray is a poet living in Aotearoa. They like cold water and being alone. They have performed their poetry in many places including Verb Wellington and the Newcastle Writers Festival. They have also represented Otago at the NZ National Poetry Slam finals. Their work has been published in *Poetry New Zealand Yearbook 2021, Landfall* and *Mayhem*. This poem was previously published in *Sport* 47 (Victoria University Press, 2019).

You've got to write like your life depends on it

You need to write like you're twenty-three but really thirty-five
with a deep obsession with Russian literature
You need to write like you're a twenty-three-year-old Libra with glossy skin
who gets horoscopes both ironically and unironically

You need to write like the internet tipped over sideways
Spilled over the last pastel gothic wedding dress found in your eccentric aunt's attic which
belonged to your even more eccentric grandmother because everyone has a story

And yours, darling
is all that matters right now

You're on the cusp of mild fame, my dear
That bewildering space where people want to know you had a girlfriend
but not what her name was
Three thousand people watching your Instagram stories

You need to write like your life depends on it

Like these sharp banalities crafted by your sardonic eye belong
in art galleries dedicated to dead poets   and poets who wish they were dead

Which is all of us crowded together
whispering eulogies and rubbing   plastic rosaries under our breath

She was a great mind gone too soon
A blistering take-down of the bucolic nightmare
Treading the edge of literary greatness

You need to write like you are already famous
but much too smart and cool to pay attention to it
Like you're the made-up girl in the leather jacket with bleached blonde hair in every movie
I've ever had a crush on who is probably based on every other person I've ever had a crush
on and sometimes when the *flick flick flick* of the screen becomes too much to bear I smash

her face in, shake the green glow and blood from my knuckles as I grasp her collar by the throat and rage-spit into her face, *Girl*

You've got to write like your life depends on it.

Ria Masae is a writer, poet and spoken-word artist of Samoan descent, born and raised in Tāmaki Makaurau. Her work has been published in various national and international literary journals including *Landfall, Cordite, Circulo de Poesía* and *Ōrongohau | Best New Zealand Poems* (2017 and 2020). Her poetry has also graced theatre productions such as *Upu Mai Whetū: Mea Fou* (2018). Ria's creative awards include first place in the 2018 Going West Poetry Slam and she was a member of the groundbreaking spoken-work team, South Auckland Poets Collective. In 2020, a collection of her poems titled 'What She Sees From Atop the Mauga' was published in *AUP New Poets 7* (Auckland University Press).

SONGS OF THE FAT WILD WOMAN

The fat wild woman
comes from a fat line of agaga faces
with brown hands who weaved intricate fala
and drummed the u'a bark for tapa
and cultivated medicine from their plantations
and cracked your legs
if you did her or hers wrong.

The fat wild woman
is a chameleon with a fat belly
that tows along Papatūānuku's skin
grounded in her glory.
Storms brew under her wild feet
as her thighs thunder across borderlines
from plantations to podiums
from village ours to lone mine
from dream messages to Christian book
to spirit of highest Self.
She can be born in a palagi land
and blend into the palagi laws
and live pockets of joy in the palagi society
but her fatu will always be wild and fat
with the spirits of her gafa.
She don't need a designer malu from palagi
tattoo parlours to CHEEEEHOOOO her belonging.
She gotsa big laugh that cuts through judgmental makas
like a sapelu through weeds of jealous faikakala
swish swish swish

fee-fi-fo-fum
I smell the blood of a coloniser
fell on his head, now he be dead
when he realised we all bleed red

The fat wild woman
she be mighty Extra.
extra-ordinary
extra-vagant
extra-vert
extra-ct-able
extra-terrestrial
cos she outta this world, baby.

But sometimes
even the fat wild woman
get burnt by spitfire jokes
sometimes she don't feel so wild
sometimes her brown skin wear paper thin
and the sticks and stones tremors her poise
sometimes the upu needle her heart
and she stands in front of her palagi mirror
that hangs on the palagi wall in her palagi house
and stops singing
like it's over.

Natalya Tongotea has whakapapa to Ngāpuhi and Ngāi Tahu, as well as having affiliations with the village of Pangai, Tonga. **Kat Taufalele** hails from the villages of Ta'anea, Vava'u and Fanga 'o Pilolevu, Tonga. The iconic duo were introduced to spoken-word poetry by their English teacher Mr Thomas [Sir]. They've competed in Counties Manukau White Ribbon, Kate Edger Educational Charitable Trust and WORD – The Front Line competitions (2014–2018). Their work has been published in *Poetry New Zealand Yearbook 2019* and *Craccum* (2021). In these spaces, they continue to invoke waves of change as young Pasifika women.

Adolescent Rhymes

Eenie

Meenie

Miney

Mo

Catch a tiger by their toe if she squeals

DON'T

You let her go

Eenie Meenie Miney

no

No

NO

It's *funny* how 'no' has become slang for 'yes'

a quick abbreviation said to save time,

No . . . doesn't mean no protection

No means protect me

From unwanted ropes of

predatory selection

Eenie Meenie Miney MO

It's *funny* how the knots we tied as kids

looped the loop too many times

and now
we're the ones tripping over them

Our bunny ears, *chains* around our throats

While salivating *tongues*

are bound by tangled thoughts

We say what you want to hear

but you weren't taught any better

Better have stayed at home

right?

Better have covered up more right?

Better have chosen a different path

right?

Because red lights wouldn't stop you

Red capes never held you back

I never wanted to be your matador

breaking china stores was not enough for you

your hunger blocking out the beacon of my red

hood

Like streetlights blocking out the stars heavy eyelids
eclipsing full moons

'Oh my, what big eyes you have'

Words trapped in deaf-eared cages skin thick but bone deep,

'Oh my, what big ears you have'

As yellow bricks bled dirt and grime into the gaps
in between your teeth

'Oh my, what big teeth you have'

and I can see myself in them.

Tick Tock

While boys were learning how to count

WE had *learnt* to count ourselves lucky

Tick Tock

Tick Tock

Hickory Dickory Dock
the mouse went up the clock
the clock struck one

in five because for one in five their time will come

Tick Tock

The clock's hands the only pair reaching out

Tick Tock

Teachers never listened to us

Tick Tock

when we told them that we already knew

That girls were not meant to walk alone at night

that if we think we're being followed

pretend to be on the phone

That our skirts should be lower than our knees

and our shirts higher than our collarbones

That boys were supposed to ask first

but did they?

Tick Tock

After all it isn't the teacher's fault if the student fails

But if the student never learnt the lesson

then who's to blame?

Tick Tock

If he follows me at night

Tick Tock

When old men prey on little girls

Tick Tock

When nursery rhymes and fairy tales

make things sound

so

so sweet

Tick Tock

If he never asked first

Tick Tock

Tick Tock

Tick Tock

Tick Tock

Then who's to

blame?

Olivia Hall (she/her) is a performance poet from Tāmaki Makaurau with a Masters in Gender. She has won poetry slams in New Zealand, New York and London, including being the 2019 Genesis Champion and competing in the finals of the NZ and UK national competitions. Olivia's poems have been published in *Catalyst*, *The Spinoff* and *Poets Versus Sexual Harassment*, an anthology with UN Women in the UK. Alongside Carrie Rudzinski, she is the co-creator of two poetry theatre shows – *How We Survive* (2019) and *Hysterical* (2022), the latter of which won Best New Play at the Wellington Theatre Awards and Outstanding Performance Poetry at the Auckland Fringe Festival.

The Skinny List

For five years I kept my own
special kind of bucket list.
It was my 'Things I'll Do When I'm Skinny' list.

My 'Bike Around Amsterdam in Booty Shorts' list.
My 'Own Skinny Jeans and a Bikini' list.

It was my 'One Day I'll Be Beautiful' list.
And my 'Then I Will Start Living' list.
It was a 'Maybe I Can Be Worth Something' list.

So each night I sat and imagined a tool
that would let me carve layers
off my body. I imagined cutting
off pieces of me and giving them to boys
in the hope that if they could not love
all of me, maybe they could at least love
part of me. Maybe that would be easier
to swallow.

And still I kept the list.
When I am skinny, I will
take my clothes off before sex.
When I am skinny, I will
do the heart breaking.

I lived eternally torn
between wanting to love myself
and wanting to lose myself.
I carved the word 'enough'
into my thigh, because I only felt

worthy of love letters
that caused pain and compliments
that made me bleed.

But it turns out hating your own body
is exhausting, especially when
the rest of the world is already
doing it for you. So one day
I put that list in a drawer and started trying
to unlearn all the problematic things we teach
about bodies. See, I was raised to believe
that compliments on my thinness
would satisfy any hunger.
Body shaming was my bible
but I know we can teach something better.

So, I stopped longing for boys
who could only love me
skinny and started longing for boys
who were better
instead.

I re-watched all the Disney movies I loved
as a child, but this time I made sure to notice
that Ursula was just as hot
as Ariel.

I re-read the Harry Potter books,
and I imagined Hermione as a fat girl,
and it didn't change what a badass heroine
she was or the fact that everyone in that series
would have died without her.

I realised that envying other girls' bodies
didn't make me any happier,
and their beauty didn't have to take away from mine.

I tried to forget every time this body
has been made to feel worthless
and started focusing on the fact this body
is my living, breathing miracle
instead. I stopped pinching and scratching
this stomach and these thighs
in favour of tracing gentle lines over my stretch marks
and thanking these legs for not shaking
when I speak the truth.

And somewhere, among all of this,
it happened.

Teaching myself to love other fat bodies
made me finally, finally start to fall in love
with mine.
One day I looked down at my 'Skinny List'
and all I saw was a bucket list.

That night, I stood in front of the mirror
and said *I am enough, I am enough*
until it didn't hurt anymore,
and it was the love letter
my body deserved.

Penny Ashton began performing poetry in 2002 and has since taken her comic feminist spoken word all over the globe, from the Edinburgh Festival to Glastonbury, to NYC's Bowery, to representing Australasia in a Slam Tour of the UK, to two Billy T. James Comedy Award nominations. She initiated Auckland Writers Festival's Poetry Idol, which ran for ten years, and now runs the WOMAD Poetry Slam. Penny regularly tours her solo literary musicals *Promise and Promiscuity* (2013) and *Olive Copperbottom* (2017), and is a playwright, social commentator, celebrant and podcaster who met her husband, fittingly, at a poetry gig.

The Angry Poem

*A response to a heckler in a comedy club telling me to lose weight, and to the wondrous woman who called him a c**t on my behalf.*

Friday Night 10 p.m.
Stag do loosed from the control of hens
Stumbles into my gig
Determined to prove just how big
A man you really are
Fuelled with amber from the bar
Till all sense is pissed away
And you think it would be a good idea to say
Something smart about my weight
Which I think is just great
I mean you must be a bronzed Adonis
If you think you can admonish
Someone who can't see you
What a brave thing to do
Yelling out from a darkened crowd
Mistaking funny for being loud
I mean some women think all men are bastards
But personally I'm ecstatic a fuck-knuckle who's plastered
Has given me something to aspire to
Man I really admire you
It's so much more interesting to hide with your mates
Than to open yourself up, becoming bait
Writing material, singing songs
Trying to connect with this Christchurch throng
Of punters and munters and pissed-up grunters
Who just coz I'm up here think they're big-game hunters
Aiming their testosterone darts at some slapperWhereas IF I WERE A MAN MY APPEARANCE WOULDN'T MATTER
Well thanks very much Mr Cunty-Cunt face
I'll remember what you said, your thought won't be erased
I'll take on board those words of grace
Then shit them out all over your face

But . . . I guess you usually probably pay for that pleasure
And now that I think what I want beyond all measure
Is for you to be completely ignored
Blanked, defunct, an entity void
I don't want to give you the satisfaction of thinking your words have any traction
On my self-esteem
You're just a wet dream
An immature ejaculation on my plastic Rubenesque sheet
And nothing you could say would make me incomplete
And yes . . . OK . . . maybe you picked a scab
Off a wound I've had
And picked since I was sixteen
But that's MY scab and MY wound and they make up me
And you HAVEN'T earned the right to that currency
And besides, if I had the choice of who I'd rather be
Then one hundred FUCKING times over I would ALWAYS pick me.

RikTheMost (they/them) is a queer, non-binary, polyamorous, pansexual, vegan spoken-word artist who spends most of their spare time making homophobes feel uncomfortable. Originally from the UK, Rik moved to Aotearoa in 2017 and has since gained residency through the prestigious Exceptional Talent in the Arts visa. They have been commissioned by the BBC, published by *Write About Now*, toured internationally, placed second three times at the NZ National Poetry Slam finals, represented Australia and Aotearoa on the world slam stage and they are New Zealand Poetry Society's vice president. Rik also runs the online poetry community Your Place Events.

Which?

He approaches:
Part human,   part whisky glass;
Both halves   are empty,
          With a question to ask.
Jim Beaming grin splashed across face,
Melting   eyes   cube   stare
Dripping at   all   *two* of us,
                                        He spills:

'So which one of you is the man and which one is the woman?'

And I want to warn him,
Before I begin:
It is not uncommon
For the venom
Of an animal
To be used
In medicine.
By this I mean:
I feel no guilt in spitting, biting, full-force injecting my answers into you
Because it's a healing;
I'm helping!
But there will be no spoonful of sugar here,
I'm not Mary-*fucking*-Poppins.

I want to show him all the poems I have written about how scary it can be:
Presenting femme,
Being non-binary;
The staring, the intimidation, the purposeful misgendering;
I want to tell him:
I have shared more vulnerability than you have 'fragile' in your masculinity.

So you'll forgive me for insisting,
Before I reply,
You consider:

Which part of you does this affect?
And,
Why do you need to know?
Actually, just try to say,
How will my answer help you?

Because if you can't,
You *curious cat*,
To continue this interaction would be unwise,
And that's not a threat to kill you,
But I may well hurt your *felines*.

You see,
I love: the way *they* look at me,
Like I am the horizon,
And not just a place between two set things,
But also the space that joins them.

I love: the feel of *their* skin
When I am kissing *them*.
The way it slightly, lightly tightens,
As if to pull me closer in.

I love: *their* mind,
So infinitely different from mine,
And not because *they* are masculine or I am feminine,
But because *they* are a beautiful, individual being
Teaching me all about that which I am not to make me more of who I am.

Can you understand what that feels like?

I wonder what narrow definitions of gender you are measuring by . . . is it:
Who is braver?
Can down a pint quicker?
Is more sensitive?
Has the better personal hygiene?
Softer skin?
Instead of crying, punches things?
Because I can assure you none of those have ever
Been relevant to our gender!

But, I fear what you're asking here is something far simpler . . .

Who fucks whom?
Who's the bread? Who's the filling?
Sand-which of us is entering or being entered in?
The fact is: we don't care, as long as everybody's eating.
And to be honest,
You sound like you're starving.

But, hey – I get it;
I understand the problem:
Dicks are difficult!
Because, like your nose and opinions,
They're always feeling forced to find somewhere they can be *put in*.
But this time,
Why not try your own arse, mate?
You might even enjoy it, maybe.
Tell me, where does that fit into your sense of masculinity?

Sorry, I'm making all sorts of assumptions about *you* now, aren't I?
Fancy that!
Let's get back to the question, right?
Basically, what you are asking is:

What do our genitals look like?

Which, when put *that* way,
Is a *bit* of an odd greeting . . .

So I don't answer any of these things;
No, I am not here to be your teacher.
Which one of us is the man and which one is the woman?
I proudly reply,

'Neither.'

Performance poet, journalist and creative nonfiction writer **Simone Kaho** was the 2022 Creative New Zealand Emerging Pasifika Writer in Residence at the International Institute of Modern Letters (IIML) at Te Herenga Waka Victoria University of Wellington. She directed the *E-Tangata* web series *Conversations* and wrote poetry collections *Lucky Punch* (Anahera Press, 2016) and *HEAL!* (Saufo'i Press, 2022). Her connection to poetry culture began at the Poetry Live open mic in Auckland. After performing as a guest poet for the first time, Simone submitted her poems to the IIML and was successful. Simone's all-time favourite performance was in a white manaakitanga tent during the land protest at Ihumātao in 2018, with Pania Newton in attendance, in the middle of a winter storm.

This poem was first published in *HEAL!*

. . . young families, with children.

The overnight rain stops before I wake up and go walking.
A blue ball is sitting in wet grass; kids live around here.
It matches your eyes and the dress I wanted to wear tonight but I need to buy it first
Jasmine is choking out the natives in the creek under the bridge down the street, where we used to hang out and look at the naked lady painted on the tree trunk, that also looked like a devil head on some angles.
Her outstretched arms, horns, and her crotch a pointy chin.
She's gone now, and the trunk has split in two, although the tree is still alive.
Half of the trunk has sent out thin branches that quiver like whips in the morning chill.
Everyone I love has died in one way or another but it's spring.
I died too, to make way for something new, and we can call it spring.
Blossoms swimming in the veins of trees all winter are emerging.
My neck still needs a scarf, but the most tender petals are out, white and pink
like little girls' faces.
In the kōwhai tree, whose branches are the colour of my face, tūī are getting delirious.
I meet an old lady at the Coffee Project getting my almond flat white.
She licks her KeepCup and talks about how the *Islanders* moved into Waterview after the *old people* who used to live there *died off.*
She says, *Islanders*, with narrowed eyes and a pause.
Anyway, she smiles and licks.
Spit glints in the air.
It's changed again.
Now it's young families, with children.

Zech Soakai is of Samoan and Tongan descent and hails from Poutasi, Falealili, Samoa and Ha'ato'u, Ha'apai, Tonga. He is also a proudly Palmerston North-born and South Auckland-raised son of the Moana. An orator, educator, village builder and warrior raiser, Zech is committed to raising a generation of truth-tellers and edge-walkers. Participant on the 2018 Rhodes Poetry Retreat and cast member of poetry theatre shows *Skin* (2014) and *Mouth: Tongue: Teeth:* (2017), he is also winner of the 2016 University of Auckland Poetry Slam and 2017 GROUNDED: Battle of the Arts. Zech's solo poetry was featured in the Auckland War Memorial Museum exhibition Pou Kanohi (2017) and, under the poetry collective Niu Wave, he released the spoken-word poetry short film *When We Speak* (2017).

Hood Questions

I'm thinking of the young men I teach.
The music they listen to
how some might say it glorifies violence
and it does.
But I say that art imitates reality, and
somewhere in the verses and the melodies
we see how trauma manifests itself.

It's layered
of course
as all things always are,

but does the responsibility lie on the artist, who is just a mirror to society?
Or to the young people who have never felt like those in the system
have their back?
Who have never felt like those in the system have actually seen their brown ochre faces?

Systems cannot fail those they were never meant to protect.

How is it possible that we raise entire communities who are both
invisible and hyper-visible?
Seen and unseen?
The first people you see at the detention hall in the morning
but who are never there at the prizegiving by night.
When education is the thing that tells the world what a country values
how do we value those who turn up
when they have every reason not to?

Is the responsibility on us, the passers-by?
Those in proximity to the blood and the bleeding?
Those with all the opinions and observations and the degrees on the wall?

The ones that say, 'We know a thing or two about a thing or two,'
so we sit
cooling off our double-shot espressos with a side of oat milk
and write up yet another report for the ministry
and then we high five ourselves
chanting, 'He waka eke noa'

not knowing that we may be on the same sea.
But we are on very different waka.

Or is the responsibility to the ones who take up space and say,
'I understand, actually
my husband is Samoan,
so talofa.'

Systems cannot fail those they were never meant to protect.

You know,
they know us for our trauma before they know us for our joy.
I know
that they want us to look at the colour of our skin as the barrier
when the barrier is white supremacy.

Margins and centres
violence and cycles
and us
who are born on the precipice.

They call us snowflakes,
say we partake in the oppression Olympics
a circle-jerk of who's got it worse.

The truth is,
it's probably a bit of everything, aye.
We can be complaining
and we can be tired
and we can be exhausted

and we don't have to be inspirational
to have someone to listen to us.

The truth is messy,
and I'm not qualified to speak on it
and I don't want to speak on it
but maybe
freedom and excellence is still achievable for all my students?

Maybe it's not all a conspiracy,
not just a hoax
choosing to teach every day,
full well knowing that education is just another scam,
just another way to chain us down into debt – at best –
or just another pipeline to prison – at worst.

Systems cannot fail those they were never meant to protect.

It has been almost two years since I've known one of my students
    – he is a quiet whisper of a man –
and I just got told that his dad is in prison for manslaughter.
It is no wonder that learning, for him, is not possible
when he is both fracture and fracturing.

What I do know to be true is,
that the system does things to our young brown men.
What I also know to be true is
that this world does not know how to hold us
    – any of us.
Either all laughs and jokes
    or too intimidating in our posture.
Where is the space and time to be gentle,
    in a world that expects you to be so hard?
How can one share the warmth of the sun,
    when all they have known is its absence?
Why do we watch the child that we pity
    become the adult that we're intimidated of

and we punish him for it.

Keep pushing out stats and figures,
as if there was a lack of stats and figures to show
that child poverty is the number one cause for poor life decisions.

We speak of emotion but only ever through the filter of white voices
    our rage, just a caricature to be laughed at on *Police 10/7*
    our grief, looked at as an economic liability,
because what they don't understand is
    that 'ofa and fa'alavelave are sometimes the same thing.
That love and responsibility are sometimes the same thing.

How thick must one's privilege be,
to make one so blind?

        Specsavers don't have spectacles for that kind of myopia.

Where I work,
inequity is the oxygen and poverty is the mother tongue.
Where I work,
my students are told that dreams belong to those where the hill
is the colour of rose petals
and that nothing good can come from this hood.
Where I work,
a reliever calls a Year 9 white trash
but is not interrogated as to how
my classroom is almost burnt down into ash.

But we laugh, laugh, laugh,
and play our siren jams
and we punch, punch, punch
and finish school early when it rains.

If you're asking me,
this ain't luxury
but your pity is also cheap.

And
they were half right
if their idea of good is them,
then, nothing good
comes from this hood.

Systems cannot fail those they were never meant to protect.
But Angela Davis might have been right when she said,
'You have to act as if it is possible
to radically transform the world,
and you have to do it all the time.'

So in spite of everything I already know
I say what my students once taught me to say,
I say,
Leeessshhggooo!

Jai Ngaranoa Selkirk is an artist whose blood shares the currents of the Northern Wairoa River in Takiwira. Laced with his signature wordplay and witticisms, Jai's poetry encapsulates the complexities of his lived experiences – a theme that resonates across the various stages where his stories have received acclaim. These performances include WORD – The Front Line and the Trans-Tasman Poetry Slam (winner of both in 2017), NZ National Poetry Slam finals (2020), *Dirty Passports* (2021), *A Slice of Southside* (2022) and *Verses in Visions: Truths of Tamaki* (2022). He has also performed as a featured poet for numerous conferences, competitions, workshops and open mic nights.

Missed Take 44

On Sunday they met us, they met us in medicine.
I met a force of mental walls of metaphors.
I met a fork in the road, for the fourth week in a row.
You fall weak before you can reap the seeds that we sow, desperately want.
So what do we want?
And when do we want it?
Really, I just want to be more than a one-hit but too bad I'm half illiterate.
I tried to clean up my act but I talk too much rubbish I litter it.
My methods worked for a little bit.
Just for a little bit.
Worked for the hard workers and the ones who wore war on their sleeves.
The ones who stay quiet, a treaty.
The trees don't die if no one saw.
Like the meteors that killed the dinosaurs or the media that kills us all in law.
All in all
It was only the sidewalks there to catch us when we fall.
The way that we meet let-downs say that we've been here before.
For the expectations that we didn't meat like a herbivore, and for all of the excuses that we've heard before,
We say fuck it
And move onto the next
Because you can't get ahead without aiming for the neck.
Near misses are mistakes from misheard gremlins turned sessions into their methods of medicine.
I met sin in medicine.
It took a trip in my mental state where my mind's cheap in real estate, but we stay in mind because we're still men till we ain't.
Misguided, missed exits and misdirection.
All the drive in the world and I still missed the destination.
Is it enough for us to miss in the midst of it?
Mist in your expression
Oceans on your chest but aching in your back.
Your bloody eyes in the mirror.

A cheat code the eyes, they never lie.
I saw it.
Ice in your eyesight.
It froze me.
Froze me at the point where the fro meets.
Lately I've been reminiscing.
Recently it's felt like my poetry has been a euphemism for my youth is missing.
I've choked on poetry when only the mirror was listening.
I chewed on glass in hope that everything that I spit is raw and fucking bloody.
I started earning my Pennys the Hardaway.
There wasn't much Magic a pony with one trick
And I've got nothing but war up my sleeves believing in what could have been
If I had the ego to Takeoff like Migos, and all my friends could say that I go
where he goes.
To where the sun shines and where we can let our weeds grow.
Where we grow.

Shania Pablo (they/them) began performing spoken-word poetry when they competed in WORD – The Front Line in 2015 and they have remained active in Auckland's spoken-word community ever since. Shania is a WORD – The Front Line, Rising Voices and JAFA Poetry Slam finalist. They have also coached WORD – The Front Line and have recently become a board member of the JAFA Poetry Slam.

The Immigrant's Guide to Speaking White

When you step off the plane into new land
make sure your white voice is already in your mouth

Check in the bathroom mirror to make sure that it is

Speak with a straight spine, but not too straight
Smile for every syllable that crawls past your lips

Speak in whispers, speak softly
as if cradling the person you're speaking to

Greet each person with *Hello!*
How are you?

And end each conversation with *Thank you!*
or *Have a nice*
day!

Bring your white voice to school
sounding white is synonymous with being intelligent.

Bring your white voice to your job interview.
Use it as a shortcut for success.
Save yourself from bending your back
as much as your parents have.

Use big words, but not too big!
It'll make you sound like a smartass,
and no one likes arrogant immigrants here.

Be humble. Be sweet.
Avoid being emotional at all costs.

Do not sound sad.
Do not sound angry.
If you don't sound nice then no one will listen to you.
Xenophobia runs deep here and your body is already a threat.

Use your white voice like papaya soap –
cleanse your body of the shame that shades your skin.

If that doesn't work,
then pour bleach into your vocal chords.
To counteract the taste of your accent
Everyone will thank you for it.

Don't you know that your accent is a threat, too?
That your rolled r's and sharp t's spell sacrilege in this country?

Cram your accent in a suitcase along with your culture,
and keep it in the basement.

Don't expose it to sunlight
God forbid that it grows and you dream of making it part of you again –
you know you don't belong here.

Use your white voice as a reminder that you should know your place.

Your white voice is a product of sacrifice.
Speak white until you don't sound like your parents anymore,
until they don't recognise your voice when they pick you up from school.

Speak white until your ethnicity looks less like a flag and more like a question mark.
Let people ask you where you're *from* from
and say that you're a Kiwi,
even if you don't know what that means.

Stop singing to your homeland,
speak white until you no longer dream in your mother tongue.
Knock your ancestor's teeth out of your jaw
and remember

Your white voice doesn't belong to you, it belongs to the majority
so make sure you sound how they want you to.

When you step foot before the crowd,
make sure your white voice is already in your mouth.

Run your fingers over your gums to make sure that it is.

Speak with a straight spine,   *but not too straight.*
Smile for every burial dug out in your throat.

Speak in whispers, speak softly
          as if begging for assurance from the person you're speaking to

Greet each person with   *Hello!*
                    How are you?

End each conversation with   *Thank you!*
                    Have a nice day!

          And smile,
               even when no one is watching.

爱华 ไอวา Aiwa Pooamorn is a Thai Chinese mother, writer, theatre maker, performer and home healthcare support worker. She is co-director of Creative Creatures, a feminist arts collective featuring Asian people of colour, whose 2020 theatre show *Have You Ever Been With An Asian Woman?* won Auckland Fringe's Unf**K The World Award. She was runner-up at the 2018 YWCA Auckland Spoken Word Competition and finalist at the 2018 Going West Poetry Slam. Aiwa's poems have been published in *Landfall*, *Sport* and various anthologies. She is currently an Ideas in Residence artist at Basement Theatre.

I'm Mama Aiwa

I'm mama aiwa fresh off the boat girl
I'm mama aiwa thai–chinese wife
I'm mama aiwa active on tinder
I'm mama aiwa late for kindy
I'm mama aiwa sit naughty corner
I'm mama aiwa cry roll round sandpit
I'm mama aiwa don't cook pad thai
I'm mama aiwa water native tongue
I'm mama aiwa birth 3 headed naga
I'm mama aiwa dj sailormoon porn
I'm mama aiwa no need dick
I'm mama aiwa sacred yoni
I'm mama aiwa big cunt energy
I'm mama aiwa hot pink bathrobe
I'm mama aiwa lime green business suit
I'm mama aiwa unemployed daughter
I'm mama aiwa smoke weed drink wine
I'm mama aiwa work 24/7
I'm mama aiwa japanese boombox
I'm mama aiwa muay thai champion
I'm mama aiwa johrakae fad hang
I'm mama aiwa come play mahjong
I'm mama aiwa breastfeed while I shit
I'm mama aiwa iron my cheongsam
I'm mama aiwa 1 dollar lip gloss
I'm mama aiwa party hard k rd
I'm mama aiwa tiger stripe stretch mark
I'm mama aiwa fuck bio-oil
I'm mama aiwa skinny dip dark water
I'm mama aiwa seaweed pubic hair
I'm mama aiwa nude on ladies bay
I'm mama aiwa tell white hubby shaddup
I'm mama aiwa no morning after pill
I'm mama aiwa placenta in freezer

I’m mama aiwa eat blood red whenua
I’m mama aiwa feed me mangroves
I’m mama aiwa child run wild
I’m mama aiwa follow me on insta
I’m mama aiwa 我是大妈

Jessie Fenton is a two-time NZ National Poetry Slam runner-up and an incurable show-off. She has won numerous poetry slams: from the Auckland Writers Festival to WOMAD and the Nuyorican Poets Café, and has even snuck her way into the Canadian Individual Poetry Slam. Jessie is an organiser and MC for the JAFA Poetry Slam, Tāmaki Makaurau's regional slam competition, and a coach for high-school poets through WORD – The Front Line. Her poems have been published in *Starling*, *Stasis*, *Wild Honey*, *Sweet Mammalian*, *Landing Press*, *No Other Place to Stand: An Anthology of Climate Change Poetry from Aotearoa New Zealand* (Auckland University Press, 2022) and *The Spinoff*.

TEXT ME THE *FUCK* BACK!!!!!!!!

In the time that it has taken for you to reply
I have found the Facebook page of every person you have ever talked to.
Have stalked your mother, your brother, your older sister's ex-boyfriend I know what kind of milk your great-aunt likes on her cereal, I know how your second cousin takes his tea,
Do not
Underestimate
ME.

In the time that it has taken for you to reply
I have built a monument to all of your ex-girlfriends,
pasted it with photos from their poorly privacy-protected Instagram accounts,
named it *Do You Think They Are Prettier Than Me?*
and sailed it off
into the Pacific Ocean
ABLAZE.

What are you doing with all the time in which you are not texting me, anyway?
Do you receive a nice message
and then drop your phone to the bottom of a deep, dark well
listening to hear the splash???

Do you receive a nice message
and then bury your phone beneath the shifting sands of the Sahara Desert
so you have to wait
for a hundred years
for it to surface again
before you can FINALLY reply?????????

What could you possibly be DOING
that is so IMPORTANT
that you don't have time to reply to a text that just says
Hey ;) what you up to?

HEY!!!!!!!!
WHAT THE FUCK ARE YOU UP TO???!?!??!?!??

. . .

I'm sorry.
I'm not normally like this.
It's just
I've never been very good at feigning disinterest
at being the kind of girl I know I am supposed to be.

You know – the *cool girl*.
She eats pizza but doesn't get fat
she likes to fuck but doesn't care about cuddling afterwards.

We young women have been playing this part for so long
we have distilled ~**chill*~ down into such a potent substance
that not caring has become a competitive sport.
Look at me, not upset that you forgot my birthday!
Look at me, totally laid back about being stood up!!
Look at me
a blank canvas
a clean slate
the dog you can kick because it never learned to bark back.

We are so scared of being called crazy or needy
that we don't know how to ask for what we want.
But I want more than this.

Listen.
I am not needy.
I. Have. Needs!

And if you're uninterested in fulfilling them, that's fine!
It just means maybe you and me aren't meant to be.

But if you do want to love me
you gotta love me loud
love me unapologetic
love me despite all the things that I lack.
Or at the very least,
you gotta pick up your phone
and text me the *FUCK* back.

Hadassah Grace (she/they) is a writer and performer living in Tāmaki Makaurau. She writes for and about women and the queer community and has performed across the country, from street corners to the Wellington Opera House. Her poetry was featured by the Auckland Theatre Company as part of an adaptation of George Bernard Shaw's work, and she has been published at *Vice*, *Nerve*, Radio New Zealand, *The Spinoff* and many literary journals in Aotearoa and internationally. Hadassah's debut poetry collection, *How to Take Off Your Clothes*, was published in 2019 by Dead Bird Books.

Ruined Women

You will know us by the lines
          under our eyes and across the tops of our thighs
by the smoke stains in our voices and the whisky in the words we whisper under our breath
by our lack of restraint, except the kind we keep in the top drawer of our bedside tables
by our fried brains, battered livers, and the boxes you battered us into
by the vastness of our bodies unapologetically taking up space
by our names like spitting stars and our laughs that split the room apart

You will know us by our full mouths and empty bank accounts
by the dirty plates on our floor and the toothbrushes in the depths of our handbags
by the scuffs on our combat boots and the chips in our polish
by the lipstick, and fake tan, and salt marks we leave in your sheets you will know

we are ruined women, and we are here to ruin you

We've always been here
the witches you burned because you knew we were magic
swapping our vacuum cleaners for broomsticks
          and cackling about castration under the light of the full moon
We're the girls you said were begging for it, too horny to be forced
The girls you said were damaged goods, too broken to need handling with care
the dykes who laughed at your dick and the fat girls waiting to devour you whole

our pussies have always had teeth
and we are finally ready to bite the hands that have kept us hungry

Jesus was wrong, when he went preaching on the mount
we are #blessed but we've never been meek
and we will wrestle the earth from those set to inherit it

we are the barren, bitter spinsters who are spitting out your seed
the heartless whores who scrape our wombs clean like dinner plates
the single mothers raising daughters who know how to fire a gun

we're the basic bitches on our phones in line at Starbucks
the train wrecks with pit stains on our favourite party dresses
and we haven't changed our underwear in days

we're the faces that have launched a thousand ships
the prostitutes you trapped in paint and picture frames
the cock-teasing sluts who wouldn't fuck our school's shooters
and we're not content to be your muses anymore

we are the succubus who will suck you dry
            and you are right to be scared of us
because hell hath no fury like a woman scorned
hell hath no fury like a woman fully formed
hell hath no fury like a woman

we're the 52% but we've been sleeping
too busy counting calories to count on each other
too busy carrying you to notice how strong we've grown
but we have grown so very strong

and you? You had your chance
            2000 years of chances
now we are everything you've always wanted
everything you've always feared
and we will ruin
            everything

There is great power in spoken word, and even more so coming through the lived experience of young creative **Takunda Muzondiwa** (she/her). Takunda is an actress, musician and poet from Zimbabwe, Southern Afrika. Coming from a theatre and musical background, she combines voice, drama and movement to tell stories of the heart, motherland and offer social commentary. Through poetry, Takunda expresses the importance of identity and culture as a tool for self-empowerment and strengthening communities. She is the 2022 NZ National Poetry Slam champion.

Gold. Mine.

Our continent was a gold mine
A gorging belly
We lived swollen
Throbbing at the diamond deposits in our arteries
Attracted to the soil's stars
Attraction to an audience
Torching 'UBUNTU' into the theatre drapes
We've got embers for molars
And they spark every time we soliloquy
We're mortals dancing with fire
And the world watches
Their jaws hanging
Like acrobats on a circus tent ceiling
Their eyes peeled like orange skins
Sins
Like letting the freaks of nature escape from the circus
Can never be forgiven
And I wonder
When the audience became
Puppets to the imperialists too
It seems to be a world filled with wanderers
The colonisers wandered too
From village to nation, they wandered
From nation to continent, they wandered
From continent to bodies, they wandered
Until they mastered it
The first step to siphoning a man from the body of water
That is his land
Is to
Liquidate his assets and name it water bending
Claim all his wealth and name it a fortune-telling
A foretelling
Of the fire and brimstone
To rain down upon a continent of stolen gemstones

Bait us
Then break us
Tell us you come in peace
While piercing your hand through our spine
Fine isn't it?
How your dominion needed dummies
Your conquests made by ventriloquists
Masters of puppetry
Magicians of manipulations
A ventriloquist and magician
Two sides of the same coin
No matter how many times they say
Look at the cards
Look at the cards –
Look at the contract
Look at the contract
There will always be strings attached
A ventriloquist distracts an audience
Whilst planting destruction at the heart of the puppet from behind
And the audience sits
Watching the puppet burst at the seams
Stitches unravelling
Cotton stuffing erupting from its sides like tumours
Fine isn't it
How a continent becomes known
For all its broken
All its poor
All its corruption
Without questioning who left the growth there to fester in the first place
Ventriloquists are masters at a disappearing act
So how could we ever suspect them?
The circus sadists
Who left
Mauled bodies and spirits
Dripping off the stage
Like thawing ice
It is a slippery slope to salvation
I wonder if their God is proud of what they have done here
Because if not
I would pray twice before I
Looked to the skies
And begged for forgiveness

Abby Irwin-Jones (she/her) is a bookseller, law student and proud former road patroller from Tāmaki Makaurau. She has been performing for eight years and has competed at national and international level. She is a Trans-Tasman Poetry Slam champion, a Word Up! slam champion, a WORD – The Front Line alumnus, and a finalist in the Stand Up Poetry and Going West Poetry slams. Abby is nineteen-years-ancient, a motorcycle rider and deathly afraid of butterflies.

Lady Bird
2017, dir. Greta Gerwig

When you're a teenage girl with the winning combination of being anti-social and conventionally unattractive
you unlock the special skills of using comedy as a crutch and being able to orbit conversations to look like you're part of the group without ever actually contributing

I've mastered the arts of invisibility and adapting my personality:
I cuff my jeans and tuck in my shirt,
step into the open-plan kitchen-dining area of the 5-bedroom house in Mount Eden that smells
like David Seymour and your parents' divorce papers

and suddenly I am just another one of the indie skater boys leaning on the Italian marble kitchen island chain smoking cigarettes until he chokes on the name of his favourite band but it doesn't matter cuz *'You probably wouldn't have heard of them anyway, they're like, pretty underground.'*

I am not the quirky girl in a Cotton On wrap skirt he is destined to go upstairs with
so I end the conversation with
'Tarantino's kinda problematic dude'
grab a Heineken
and strike up a conversation
with the nuclear family framed in the hallway
Victorian-villa-corridor-surrealist-art-gallery
I tell the photos of the private-schooled kids
that they are who I wanna be when I grow down
turn around
and age backwards
Benjamin Button my way back into ignorance
back into thick skin and idealism

Now I'm just a protagonist with imposter syndrome
trying to replace my lack of character development with mediocre cinematography

How many shitty upper-middle-class parties do I have to go to before my plot has any depth?

How many misadventures and tattoos do I need to have in order to become a secondary character in a coming-of-age movie?

How much do I have to romanticise my reality until the kids at the god-awful party ask me to go chase
        infinity with them?
To hold my ankles as I stand on the centre console of Josh's Toyota Corolla and rise out of the sunroof to be baptised by the streetlights
To have stones thrown at my window
To call and know that they'll answer
To be wrapped in a cinematic soundtrack so emotional it could tell *Perks of Being a Wallflower* to fuck off and it would

So if someone came along and asked me to be a misfit with them
I would hurtle into recklessness

because no one ever taught me that a youth survived was not a youth wasted

So I wait for someone to hand me a social life and a Cruiser
but they never come

Because 'Ribs' by Lorde comes on
        and they all rush to the windowsills
                climbing on the rooftop to sing at the stars
                        dancing under the moonlight
                                congratulating themselves on their individuality
                                        filling their cups and Instagram stories
                                                leaving the house empty
                                                        except for me.

A girl too bitter her life didn't work out exactly as she planned to join in

because I am only as valuable as the amount of misogynistic white boys in Doc Martens that want to sleep with me
because I am only as valuable as the amount my life reflects a storyline that ends at graduation
troped-up teens played by 30 year olds
written into existence by middle-aged men in board rooms

When's the story gonna start?
When's the opening credits gonna roll?

Someone waves at me from down the hall
but my Uber's here
so I tell the parents' wedding photo hanging by the door that
I miss them
and leave

leaving nothing but a stained-glass shadow on the hallway floor
and a hazy memory in a drunk boy's mind
of stopping on the way to the bathroom
seeing a girl in the hallway talking to the pictures on the wall
of not getting to start a conversation before she finishes her drink and leaves

He won't remember in the morning
but he thought
she was kinda pretty.

Dan Goodwin (they/them) is a Scottish Pākehā performance poet, dramaturge and writer. In 2016, they completed their Masters in Text and Performance at RADA and Birkbeck, London. A proud JAFA poet, they are the 2021 Auckland Regional and NZ National Poetry Slam champion. Their poetry has been published by *Re:*, *eel mag*, *The Spinoff*, *Attitude* and the Burnett Foundation. They have performed internationally and across Aotearoa, including at Auckland Pride, Auckland Live Cabaret Season, NZ International Comedy Festival, Bloomsbury Festival and Welcome to Nowhere. Dan most recently wrote and performed a sell-out season of their poetry-play *Chrome Dome and Schizo* at Basement Theatre.

Amen

The word *Love* is our greatest invention.
I have never known a better suitcase
for a species so bad at packing.

'I love you' is the triple pirouette of the word
Love is the jump, *you* are the landing and the magic
is in how we twirl baby twirl!

One night
while writing their wedding vows
my friends Joanne and Jessica
argue
over who said *I love you* first.

For a wedding present, I joke
Would you like a blender?
or should I hand you its receipt?

Jess stares

'Fuck off.
We're lesbians.
We don't blend things. We crush them.'

I don't know what she meant by that, but trust me . . . I felt it.
Just like my shoulder didn't see her right hook coming, but trust me . . . I felt it.

See my friend Jessica has a remarkable sense
of immediacy about her.

So when Joanne recommends postponing the wedding
she pleads
'Do I not make you happy?'

Happy

Joanne tells her,
'My darling, we do not have to prove anything.'

Happy

when Jessica threw the bouquet
like a javelin towards her sister
'Catch it bitch!'

Happy

The idea that if life has a finish line you should run towards it
fast as you can.

When Joanne passed away   at 28
we filed into the church silently
praying we could go backwards.

When someone dies   their soul escapes words   becomes solar system
memories
floating around and inside those still left alive
there is no one word to encapsulate that

'Why do these people keep saying Amen?'
Jessica asks me at the back of the church
'. . . as if it means anything.'

I tell her *Amen* is a lot like *'I love you'* but too much like *Happy*
at the same time
'They're trying.'
Amen because I wish you were here
Amen because I blame you and feel so guilty
Amen because what else is there?
Amen because RuPaul
Amen because why not?
Amen because *'Thank you   for everything.'*

When Joanne's mother sees us
She says *'God Bless'* to Jessica
like *'Please don't touch me . . .'*

When she sees Jessica, her daughter (in law)
leave,
she says *'Amen'* as in *'Thank God that's over'*

Confronting the pastor about it after
he says *'It can be hard sometimes
to receive the word of God
when we need it the most.'*

I tell him *'That's true. I'll go now.
Need to work on my right hook.'*

Outside, Jessica sitting on the steps of the church,
I realise all the words I have
are entirely inadequate.

I sit beside her.
We watch the 4 p.m. sunset go down.
I offer *'I love you'*
she nods
places it to the side for later.

We sit.
Lean in to each other.
Say nothing.

Kyla Dela Cruz is a spaghetti-loving, Auckland-based Filipino performance and page poet. She writes to navigate and celebrate the way she experiences the world around her. Kyla started sharing her stories in 2014 through WORD – The Front Line and, since then, she's been runner-up in the inaugural Justice Slam, a finalist in the NZ National Poetry Slam and won the 2016 Rising Voices Youth Poetry Grand Slam.

Tight French Braid

Backstabbing used to be what other kids did/ something we didn't
know about yet/ too busy hopscotching/ our girlhood glory/ climbing
trees/ talking about the future

I was the quiet one/ thought too much about the way my stomach spilled
over my skirt/ The only thing I liked about myself was how I could make you
laugh/ louder than our classroom on its worst behaviour/ You, firecracker/
with a tight French braid/ master impersonator of teachers we didn't like/ had no trouble
breaking the rules

The principal stressed/ the hallways were out of bounds during lunchtimes/ but
there we stayed anyway/ secretly sweating an ocean
in my pits/ convinced this was the most rebellious thing I had ever done
in my life/ it still is/ But I had never felt more untouchable/ than when I was with you

With you, I forgot the shame I carried/ in this body/ how I tried to slender
myself/ to skinny up to collarbones and ribcage/ each night/ you made me
feel safe/ comfortable/ deserving of all the mince and cheese pies of this world/ I forgot
about razor blades/ shortcut ways to get into heaven

When we were thirteen/ we didn't know how to carry this kind of young love/ on our arms/ or
realise it was worth holding onto/ before
we started to crumble

Backstabbing used to be what other kids did/ something we didn't
know the meaning of/ until we learned how to wield knives ourselves/ to spit
on the spirit of sisterhood/ betray our second language

Sometimes, the one who got away/ isn't always the boy you dreamed of marrying/
sometimes it's the girl you wished you were a better friend to/
the girl who made the hell of intermediate worth surviving for

You, firecracker with a tight French braid/ my first heartbreak/
I'm sorry that's who you became/ I know *I'm sorry* isn't good
enough/ these words can't stitch the empty space between us/ can't
band-aid our broken parts back together/ make us thirteen/ and
unbreakable again

but these words are all I have/ a smoke signal you might one day notice.

Ngaio Simmons (she/her, Ngāti Porou) is a Māori Pākehā spoken-word artist and educator born and raised on the island of O'ahu in the unceded nation of Hawai'i. In her twelve years as a writer and performer, she has represented Hawai'i at Brave New Voices and the NZ National Poetry Slam. Now permanently residing in Aotearoa, Ngaio still writes about diaspora, identify conflict and what it means to be indigenous and queer in a world that consistently rejects both. Her work has featured in *Contemporary Verse*, *Flux Hawai'i*, *Literary Hub*, *Ora Nui*, *ANMLY* and the Academy of American Poets.

Smooth

I sometimes think about the man you were supposed to be
the one I saw in photos
the one in all black who made it a point to come up to me
after my performance,
introduced himself in our language
looked me in my eyes
seemed good

I had carved you out in my mind to be
fresh fruit
pōhatu face
tikanga and all about the wāhine whai mana,
just
all I needed then,
someone who could love and play guide
at the same time,
a man
who would first see descendant,
young
flushed to the bone with home

I wanna know where to go
to scrub you off
stainless steel you from me
even if it means
I walk around full lesion,
skin gone
and growing new slowly,
I want to be shown
the right way to process you,
four years since I started therapy
and so far from being newly twenty,
I have nothing –
the writing hurts too much but it's all I have

I wish someone stopped you
I wish everyone's stomachs
and gods
and *kindness*
saw you,
split their bodies open in anguish trying to figure out
what to do *with* you
to you

Our people are not strangers

Your mother showed me our families' connections
and made you pour me a glass of milk,
your brother slipped into his gumboots
and pushed you into the nettles to make me laugh,
your father smiled wide at me
and welcomed me without question right in front of you

You
told me we would write when we got to your house,
but showed me every corner of your bed instead
'convinced' me
under the neighbourhood streetlights
that we wouldn't be seen by the houses towering over us,
spoke to me in the reo at kura
praying my tongue would fumble and fall as whaea watched on

Our people
are not strangers,
our people
knew each other
our people
knew mana when they saw it,
but you

Wāhine brought you here
yet when we count the distance from Pō to you
how far you've fallen
hitting your head on every step,
unrecognisable
to our atua
our tīpuna
our people

Only the reddest of your blood
can look and see shape but
the most sacred among us
the most mana among us

see something fading in the sand
rough outline
just smoke

No one knows you

I wish I had known this
before your hands grew fluent in Me
wish I was less afraid to be queer then
wish someone with Sight was good enough
to keep my jaw from ever meeting yours

Wish you were full form

Wish I never met you

Vex Chat-Blanc is a dancer and game designer from Taranaki who has been performing for seemingly endless years both on the floor and sometimes even standing up. Vex is currently working on a game called Hunting Billionaires For Sport. Vex longs for world peace but would settle for mutually assured annihilation.

Final Thoughts While Dying

1
This is how I always wanted to go –
Fighting a shark with my bare hands
Kicking and screaming as my limbs are sundered by fifteen rows of teeth.

2
Statistically my chances weren't good.
Every year more people die taking selfies than being attacked by sharks.
A millennial's worst sin is vanity;
Daring to love ourselves so much we would die for us.

3
Five things I will never grow up to do:
I) Become a hydra.
II) Give enough of a fuck to file a tax return.
III) Colonise Mars.
IV) Or tame any other god of war, for that matter.
V) Write a bestselling novel about an affluent white boy, who meets an eccentric blue-haired girl, who teaches him to open his heart to literally anything other than thinly veiled bigotry, all just before he's drawn and quartered by the proles in a violent insurrection.

4
This is how I always wanted to die –
Fighting a shark
For real estate.

Zephyr Zhang 张挚 is a poet and performer based in Tāmaki Makaurau whose work explores migrant and queer experiences. They are both neurodivergent and sleepy. Some spaces where they have read poetry include Verb Readers & Writers Festival, Going West Writers Festival and Basement Theatre. Zephyr recently performed in the Auckland Theatre Company iteration of *Scenes from a Yellow Peril*. They have been published in *Starling*, *Sweet Mammalian*, *Mayhem* and a range of independent zines.

red

the worn plush of a cinema chair
the smooth pen strokes of a bad grade
red sunsets
red strobe lights
lipstick and chipped nail polish

chinese new year
firecrackers and red envelopes
a flag with yellow stars
weddings and the family unit
filial piety and good fortune
a dream of red mansions

roof tiles placed on a house
a red suzuki swift parked on the lawn
a red feature wall, redwood deckchairs, a brick chimney
strawberry jam and some cordial
and a red diary inscribed with red angst

red angst and love hearts
she has red shoes and warm lips
flushed cheeks and bloodshot eyes
she is shared wine and a number three billiard ball
the cherry on top
youtube and netflix
silk pyjamas and a maroon duvet
the city link bus, beach pōhutukawa
the new zealand symphony orchestra and the auckland art gallery

I write with a red pen
words gush out from thin slit wounds
it's a diary stained with tears and blood

wolves can smell red
blood and fear
the scent of hidden secrets
sweaty palms, fermented grapes and a blood moon
like unearthing a body
uprooting a family tree
there is a gasp
then the sound of pages turning
and silence after the howl

it starts softly
why are you like this?
is it a broken family
bad parenting
1B8s in an all-girls school
too many red liquorice sleepovers
it is disobedience
it is disrespect
it's because I hate my culture
another lost daughter
it's because I talk back
and she sees red

red is the colour I spit when lips are split
when fist meets braces
when wrists are twisted
it's tough love
a bruised apple and a broken plate
a wallet with a single hundred dollar note
a bed against the door, a cabinet against the window
a red-hot poker in hand guarantees safety
get out, gun dan

if you slice me open
you will find lots of red
I bleed love!!!
roses and candy hearts
red string and red guts

a piñata is made to break
a human is made to heal
from fresh crimson to a deep burgundy
cuts stitch, hearts mend
and a red dawn heralds a new day

Te Kahu Rolleston (Ngāi Te Rangi) is a descendant of the waves that break against the shores of Tauranga Moana and he is from the islands that shelter the smooth waters of Tauranga, from the rough seas of the ocean known as Te Moana-nui-a-Kiwa. He has been called The Taniwha of Slam Poetry. Te Kahu is the 2013 NZ National Poetry Slam champion and was invited to attend the Banff Centre's Indigenous Writing Programme in 2015 alongside Witi Ihimaera. He has performed at TEDx Tauranga, appeared on numerous television shows including *Good Morning*, *I am TV*, *Pūkana* and *2Kaha*, on Radio Tainui, and he has been published in *Puna Wai Kōrero: An Anthology of Māori Poetry in English* (Auckland University Press, 2014).

Rena

So it began.
As the essence of death crept,
from the monsters' depths
unto the sand.
Impacting all creatures
from the air, sea, and the land.

She was stuck,
between a reef and a hard place.
Jammed, like my nan's boiled fruit pulp,
in a jar case.

Its knife-like features. With a sharp blade,
pierced my Moana.
Oozing and bleeding this dark paste.

She was stuck.

No anchor, no margarine, nothing but a
dark taste.
Volatility spread,
churning my once bright pantry and sanctuary
to a dark place.

We were going wild, lives spinning.
Out of control.
At the amount of wildlife killing
that was occurring.
As the government sat around, downing Caesar salads just chilling.

How dare you!!
Poison the swells and the realm of Tangaroa.

Then sit around and watch . . .
as time ticks on while doing nothing at all.
To those with the access and knowledge,
It's a food basket and store.
Payments made with the practice of kaitiakitanga, tikanga and l.o.r.e . . . law.
Until that day, when the blanket of death lay, on our sea bed and she was almost a beach
dead for shore.

I saw them . . . an army of Taniwha,
surfing the waves.
In the shape of shipping containers though nothing within them could be contained.
Armoured in steel, stealing the life of my Moana away
Unless you've been raised.
To be at one with the sea, you could never see or even believe this sort of pain.

As it happened.
There was a culture clash . . .
The classic one . . .
Money verses Mana!

Who determines or measures success and wealth?
Is wealth the ability to collect enough food to sustain yourself?
Or is wealth
forever more to be acknowledged as the assets in your possession
and cash in your bank account?

Because the sea is a resource
to practicers of capitalism.
But what's a re-source to a mauri-source,
our people's very essence of living?

When it happened we answered the sea's call.
An army of gumboots and latex gloves that protected us from nothing, believe me.
This is the sort of love and strength found among whānau, hapu and iwi.

After this tragedy. We had to find the silver lining.
The shimmer of hope we wound up identifying
was the unity that derived from such a tragedy.
That's the only reason there are still smiles on our faces.
There has to be
because to quit, is to steal hope from the next generation.

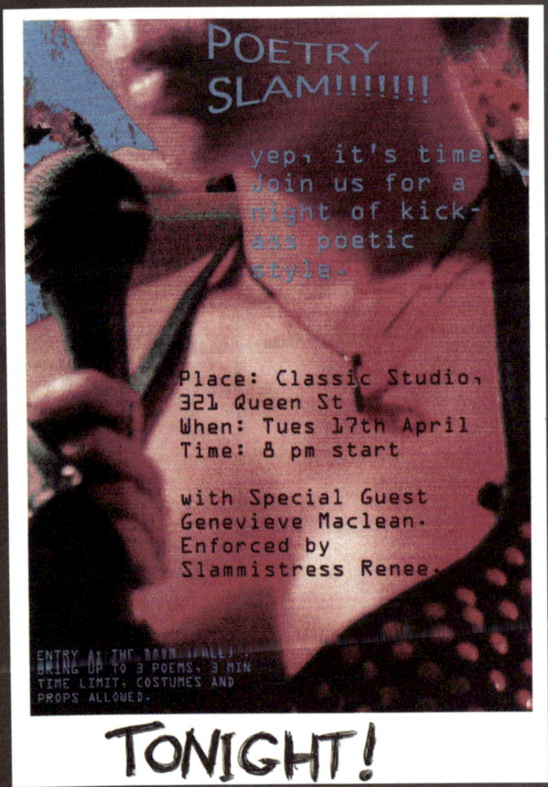
POETRY SLAM!!!!!!!
yep, it's time. Join us for a night of kick-ass poetic style.
Place: Classic Studio, 321 Queen St
When: Tues 17th April
Time: 8 pm start
with Special Guest Genevieve Maclean.
Enforced by Slammistress Renee.
BRING UP TO 3 POEMS, 3 MIN TIME LIMIT, COSTUMES AND PROPS ALLOWED.
TONIGHT!

45 cents an hour

catalystnz.blogspot.com
CATALYST ROAD SHOW
My Republic
actual books
live music
real poetry
SAT 30 AUG, 9PM
The Darkroom
336 St Asaph St
WORD CHRISTCHURCH

2

Float

Ken Arkind is a US National Poetry Slam champion who has performed his work and facilitated workshops across the world. He holds a BCA in Creative Writing from Manukau Institute of Technology and is the author of two poetry collections including *Coyotes* (Penmanship Books, 2013). Ken has appeared on multiple TEDx stages, HBO, TVNZ, Radio New Zealand and NBA.com. He is a co-founder of the JAFA Poetry Slam, co-producer of the NZ National Poetry Slam and currently works as a poet and youth development worker for Action Education, facilitating workshops across Aotearoa and co-producing WORD – The Front Line.

Michelle. Michelle. Michelle.

I'm trying to write a poem right now but I can't because I don't write poems anymore. It's been a long time. Instead all I do is 'try' to write stories about old dead friends and in a vain attempt to forget about the recently dead one.

For instance, I had a friend named Tony Blackowl when I was a kid. I wasn't a very good friend to him. In our house, my mother always gave the guest first pick. It was the polite thing to do. So naturally, when I was at his house I would expect the same, but his mother was the opposite. Tony always got the best of both worlds. The biggest slice of pizza, the piece of cake with the most frosting, Mario over Luigi.

It used to make me so angry, so I'd pick on him. I once called him my third best friend, behind James and Shane. Tony cried because I was his only friend and even that was arranged by our parents.

When I finally voiced my frustration to my mother she explained. Tony had a condition. Tony had two hearts. A large regular one, just like me. And then a smaller one that was growing inside of the first. The second heart would eventually get so big it would rupture the first and he would die, sooner than later. His mum just wanted him to have the best while he still had the chance. That's why he always got first pick of things. It's why she cried for no reason when she put us to bed.

Once, I asked him if he could feel it. The second heart. Did he have two heartbeats? Could he hear them arguing inside his chest? He said no, not really. Every once in a while he could hear a flutter, like a bird's wing. Almost as if something was trying to leave him but couldn't get out. I never knew what happened to Tony, I moved away in the third grade and we stopped talking, but I always assumed that he had died.

Mike Tyson once said, 'Everyone has a plan until they get punched in the face.' I like to use quotes in my writing because it makes me sound smarter. That was me trying to be honest.

Honesty is not always the best policy but it is my policy. Honesty is a stray dog in my neighbourhood. I leave food out for it and in the morning the bowl is empty but it never comes inside.

Honestly, I have been afraid of being a poet. Honestly, I have spent a huge part of my life telling people, telling young people, that poetry can change the world. I don't know if I believe that anymore. I have known too many dead poets.

Sometimes I smile at the thought of being a restaurant owner, or a builder. At least then what I do is immediately tangible. Like, I have fed someone, and I know this is good. I have built something that people use every day. This is good.

My friend Geoff used to be a poet that taught poetry to prisoners on Rikers Island. They did this because they wanted to change the world. After a while they got fed up and decided to become a lawyer. They believe it's a more effective way to help people

Geoff once said to me that 'There isn't a single poem in this world that can stop the State from fucking you up.' Which is true, but a poem can stand as a testament to the moments when it did. It can tell the story after the author has been silenced. I suppose that counts for something. Maybe it's just a way to tread water.

The only difference between a poem and a tombstone is whether it's written on paper or stone and then, what are monuments? Who are we carving stones for these days? Conquerors and thieves from best I can tell.

Why would I worry about writing about the dead when they are still here? When they are the most important part of our world. When all I can think about is my dead friend. The one who recently committed suicide. But that's not entirely true. When I say all I can think about is my dead friend, what I mean is that all I can think about is myself, and what I could have done differently.

Which is nothing.

That's the worst part of it. Logic tells me that I couldn't have done anything. *There is no fact in this world that can prevent a feeling from fucking you up.*

I used to write every poem like it was the poem that would change the world, like it was the most important thing I would ever do. Like I was trying to save a life.

I could tell my students to never forget to write like that. But they will. Writing the poem that saves someone else's life isn't the important part. You can't control what your poems do after they've been written. You just have to write them. The important part is being present enough to recognise the poem that saves your life.

I only know that when you write down the names of the dead, that's one more person who knew it. Too bad it isn't the opposite, that no matter how many times you say a person's name, it can't prevent them from dying.

I don't know what a poem even is. Maybe it's just a way to capture a moment in time. Like when Woody texted me a recording of the rain in Denver, a picture in words, or even a post on a Facebook timeline.

Last week while researching this story, I found Tony Blackowl's Facebook page. Laughing, and alive. The flutter in his heart grown into a son, standing next to him on a green lawn. I knew that the story I was writing about him did not save his life, that my will and memory had not raised him from the early grave he was promised. But it didn't stop me from opening my notebook and writing down the names of every person I love, over and over, until my fingers went numb.

Maggie Leigh White (Ngāti Kahungunu ki Te Wairoa, Ngāti Hinemihi, Pākehā) is a poet, performer and painter based in Kapiti. As an actor she has performed throughout Aotearoa, Australia, London and Prague in a variety of genres from Shakespeare to butoh and physical performance. Maggie has been performing her own poetry at open mics and zine launches throughout Te Whanganui-a-Tara since 2017. Her writing explores her identity as a wahine of Māori and Pākehā descent, and her connection to people, place and the natural world. Her work has been published in *Salty* and *saltwater love*.

Ngā Au

Swimming weightless
held breath //
held
in the lap and swell
of Hinemoana //
her groan and song
pushing and pulling
my rolling roundness
rippling flesh
like a million tiny fish beneath my skin //
her offspring
a shoal wet and writhing // rising to
sea foam
about my shoulders
a hissing korowai
that tastes like salt
and the cries of birds
swallowed whole in one
watery breath //
te hā o te wai
te au o te wai
ngā au // mists, smoke, rapids
currents //
ko au // me, I
unfixed
uncontainable
a flowing thing //
the wake of a waka
hauled to land
at the arrival //
the drip dripping hull
and glistening oars

she clings to them as memories of currents and spray
ko au //
walking weight-full ashore
cracked shells underfoot
salt
on my eyelashes
and an atua
dripping from my hair

Hala Nasr is an Egyptian feminist, born and raised in Aotearoa New Zealand. She has performed poetry solo and alongside the DECOLONISE poetry collective (co-founded with Jahra Wasasala and Logan Dobson) at major events in Tāmaki Makaurau including Pasifika Festival and Auckland Fringe. Hala's work is featured in the anthology, *We Call to the Eye and the Night: Love Poems by Writers of Arab Descent* (Persea Books, 2023).

To death, we crawl

Can you diagnose death?
There, then spent
like soil sitting beneath fingernails
like the angle of the earth spinning
like my restless wail at the end of a hospice
corridor
like a gasp followed by the still.
Tell me, does it hurt when our blood rests and we
are absorbed into the universe?
There's a reason breathing is enforced,
inevitable, then disappears.
But it beats me.
I'm tired of meaning, unlike the trees.
They love the clutter,
a gathering of bark, leaves, fungi, birds, worms.
They hold vigil.
Will they judge our arrogance, marking dates on
calendars?
Will they hold our hope and our hands when our
time is there, then spent?

Kiri Piahana-Wong is a poet, editor and the publisher at Anahera Press. She is of Ngāti Ranginui, Chinese and Pākehā ancestry. In her early poetry days, Kiri was a keen slam competitor and open mic reader, and an MC at Poetry Live for six years. Her poems have appeared in over forty journals and anthologies including *Essential NZ Poems* (Godwit, 2014), *Landfall, Tātai Whetū: Seven Māori Women Poets in Translation* (Seraph Press, 2018) and *Vā: Stories by Women of the Moana* (Tatou Publishing, 2021). She has one full-length collection, *Night Swimming* (Anahera Press, 2013), and a second, *Give Me an Ordinary Day*, is forthcoming. Kiri lives in Whanganui with her family.

In the mountains

You say your tūpuna always
speak to you in the mountains.
You see their faces crowding the peaks.
The snow falls on your face and
you say 'Kia ora, snow.'

I stand around taking photographs
of you and getting cold. You
want to walk further up the mountain
so I say yes and I follow
you.

We come down the mountain and you
want to drive up the other side, and
you are the one driving, driving my car,
so I say yes and soon I am following you again.

This time, when I say 'I'm cold,'
you take my hand and put your
arm around me.

Once I remember you told me
that when a girl says 'I'm cold,'
what she really means is, 'I want
you to touch me.'

This passes through my mind
when I feel your fingers clasp
mine, but actually, I am very
cold and now that your arm is
around me I don't feel as cold
anymore. You are as big as a
mountain yourself, at least twice

as big as me, so you block
the wind quite effectively.

It's strange when you are with
someone and on the one hand,
you feel safer than you have
ever been, and on the other,
as close as your clasped fingers,
you feel the abyss yawning beneath
you, black rocks tumbling away,
a cataclysm of snow falling,
a terrible noise, and then, in
the even more terrible silence
afterwards, a cloud of kāhu
lifting, speaking to me in the
voices of my tūpuna, and saying

This man is the one for you, it's meant, we want the children.

*It is going to hurt you, that's too bad, you are strong, you know
what to do with pain, stop complaining about the opportunities
you are getting.*

Because I am a complicated person,
but brought up well, I listen to my
tūpuna when they speak to me.

Even if what I am longing for
them to say, with everything I
have left in me, is

*Whakarongo mai, child,
you have had a hard time of late.*

Kāore he āwangawanga, it's all going to be just fine.

We foresee great riches in your future.

*You will meet a man, fall in love with him, he will adore you and
together you will raise beautiful tamariki for the benefit of your people,
yourselves, and your country; you will successfully mix politics, poetry
and pleasure, upgrade your Toyota Corolla to a Lincoln Town Car, and
never eat McDonald's again except when you truly want to be unhealthy.*

Ka – pai.

It was a long drive home and
I fell asleep while the black miles
rolled away and I trusted you to
keep me safe. You may not be great
at giving me the things I most need
but at least you know how to drive a car.

When I said goodbye to you, it
didn't feel like goodbye. Our
friendship is like this poem,
it could easily go on forever,
but at some point it will need to
change, or to stop, because there
is a time limit.

Don't make me wait too long, Tiori.
I am tired of being strong and sensible.

Rosanna Raymond a.k.a. Sistar S'pacific is an innovator of the contemporary Pasifika art scene as a long-standing member of the art collective the Pacific Sisters and the founder of SaVĀge K'lub. Rosanna has achieved international renown for her performances, installations, body adornment and spoken word. She is a published writer and poet, and her works are held by museums and private collectors throughout the UK, US, Canada, Australia and New Zealand. In 2022, Rosanna participated in the Hawai'i Triennial with the Pacific Sisters, and the Healing Gardens of Bab for the Fierce Festival in Birmingham with SaVĀge K'lub.

PulOtu PollUtion (Part 3)

Lights off and . . . just hit downtown *Lalolagi* . . . life under the clouds

On my way to *Pulotu* to catch up with the *tīpuna*, some old friends and the gods

Took me a while, the entrance is blocked with a global gathering of corporate-sponsored rubbish, it's mainly plastic and ocean-going.

Desecration, Testament, Treatment, Excreta

The sound of money markets and the smell of fried chicken drowning out the *tangi* of the Blood Clot, sitting patiently at the doorway, with her legs crossed and a club in both hands, chewing kava . . . her *Malu* clinging to the posts of the house

At the doorway there's a flying fox nailed onto a stick . . . Jesus styles . . . or is that spread eagle, can't make up my mind . . . anyways . . . ever get the feeling you've been shafted

No wonder the rocks and earth were weeping

I had to go the back way through Hawaiiki

Hawaiiki Nui, Hawaiiki Roa, Hawaiiki Paomaomao

The Long White Cloud led the way . . . followed by the cry for the dead

The *malofie* were there waiting to check me in . . . my passport to *Pulotu* etched on my legs

I stop and talk with some old souls, we *hongi*, they see I am a little anxious

They tell me 'Don't worry babe, *Hine-nui-te-pō* has told all the necessary bodies, the salt-water *whānau* are coming from all over the *moana*, they are weaving fine white mats and binding bundles of fuzzy limed hair.'

Blood Clot's *Malu* spies me and comes to speak to me.

I do as I am told, put my hands in the air, and drop my skin in one of the puddles

The *tatatau* didn't go, it's deeply scored in my flesh, highlighting all the spaces in between.

I have come prepared . . . I gift her a bunch of red feathers, some necklaces I made for dancing and praying and a couple of London-based *taniwha*, one is half lion half serpentine, the other a shapeshifter, she is used to the muck and mirth of mankind, she even copulates with them

They bring a bottle of single malt scotch, some old magic charms made of red coral and acorns.

All good ingredients for a soul shake down party . . . everybody turns inside out, dancing and praying, all at the same time.

Out come the guitars and the wood drums . . . gonna be one of those sing-song . . . long nights . . . no room for wallflowers here . . . everybody got to get their arse on the dance floor

We sing songs of redemption and reciprocity.

In comes the light, it shines so bright you can see into the corners of everybody's heart.

No secrets, no lies, the shadows take flight

This is paradise baby, no heaven, no hell . . . I feel quite shiny . . . all warm and fuzzy and covered in the dust and the detritus of eons of past lives.

Well as you can imagine . . . I've lost all sense of time and space . . . and when I finally get back to *Lalolagi*, it's still dark . . . looks like I'm the last one back, so better go turn on the light.

Talk about the need to be switched on

Daren Kamali is a Fijian, Wallisian, Futunan and Scottish poet and multi-disciplinary artist whose works are inspired by his upbringing in Fiji and Aotearoa. His creations draw from people and places, particularly cities, islands and the ocean. His work calls on Pacific heritage and tradition in a narrative that is fresh and vividly contemporary even as it remains strongly connected to the past. He co-founded the South Auckland Poets Collective in 2008 and founded the Street Poets & Artists Collective Enterprise (SPACE) in 2021 – working with former rough sleepers at Auckland City Mission Te Tāpui Atawhai and Auckland Council to publish a poetry anthology, *Rough Lives Speak*, in 2022.

Con-olized

We weren't Col-onized –
We were – Con-olized –
Con-d-Alive –
Our culture and language left for dead.

What a feeling that must've felt?
Standing there on Waitangi grounds
Looking at foreigners out at sea
Coming to claim newly found islands.

Ocean waves break silence on shore –
Birds sing waiata of long ago –
Swaying pōhutukawa branches –
Reminds me of kula birds from Lau.

I imagine explorers licking their top lip
Sticking a flag in the sand – on a stick
Did they really discover this land?
Tangata whenua were here already – weren't they?

Brought their muskets and cigars –
Paper and ink –
Wrote the Treaty on how they should treat us.
Treated us like human meat.

Traded nails for almost anything –
Brought clothes and shoes for us to wear –
Taught us to read the Holy Book
Now they read fiction with almost nothing to wear.

Were we Colonized or Con-olized?
Brainwashed by holy water
Hypnotized by your sweet words, thoughts – and desire
Give up your lands or die in the line of fire

What a feeling that must've felt?
Way back then
How does it still feel?
Now.

Jess Holly Bates (they/them) is a queer Pākehā artist, poet and theatre maker in Tāmaki Makaurau. Their theatre show *Real Fake White Dirt* was awarded Best Writing at NZ Fringe and was published as a book of poetry by Anahera Press in 2014. Jess has won the Page-2-Stage NZ Society London Award and toured the UK, Australia and New Zealand. They co-created two theatre works: *The Offensive Nipple Show* (2016) and *Inheritance* (2019) – the former winning Best in Theatre at the Sydney Fringe and the Tiki-Tour Ready Award at NZ Fringe. Their other career highlights include TEDx Auckland, *Nar//Scissors* (2015) and having their essay, 'An Impossible Sexuality' (2017), published in *The Pantograph Punch*.

Real Fake White Dirt

we stand on real fake grass
                                        and eat real fake butter
                                        they lodge real fake claims
                                        and aim real fake guns in the urewera
we vote on real fake flags
                                        in our real fake house
                                        giving real fake funding
                                        to those who need it
                                        most
and in our real fake māori
                                        we sing our real fake anthem
                                        letting real fake all blacks
                                        sell me biscuits
                                        if they're handsome
we put a real fake welcome
                                        at our auckland airport,

                                        a karanga on
                    pre-record

it clocks a country
                                              caught

                                              by its tits on a fish
                                        hook
                    we are dropping
                                                                              history
                    like your keys
                    into a bowl
                    so you can get drunk
                                                            on the present
                    and remember not to
                                                                              swim

home in it

***

it is a slow
slow work
embarrassing
unflattering
it is a slow
slow
work
to keep calling
and calling
and calling
and calling
and calling
the whites of your eyes
to roll back from your head

and collect your warrior clothes
pākehā

think they're on the washing
line
where you left them

Ben Fagan (Pākehā) is from Te Matau-a-Māui Hawke's Bay and Te Whanganui-a-Tara Wellington. He has shared his work across the UK, US and Aotearoa, including two poetry shows at the Edinburgh Festival Fringe. Ben's work has been featured in *The Listener*, *Newsroom* and *The Spinoff* and he has published two poetry collections, *Some Traveller* (Bx3, 2017) and video series *Pākehā 2020* (2020). He co-founded national spoken-word organisation Motif Poetry Ruri Tūtohu, has been a guest curator of Verb Readers & Writers Festival, and works with NZ National Poetry Slam, National Youth Drama School, NZ Fringe and Choirs Aotearoa NZ. Ben lives in Island Bay with his young family.

Regular 91

I say g'day to the boy with braces at the BP. As Regular 91 fills the tank I lower my voice until it's idling, I want to impress. Nah no receipt mate, cheers, yup, cheers. The ritual holds fragile.

He seems resentful of Hastings, his uniform, his acne. 'In certain towns, no matter what you've got on, you're a bad dresser . . . . Some places you're better off just moving instead of changing.' That's a line from Jerry Seinfeld's book, the kind of thing I thought was deep when I was younger. It's bad for your skin, petrol. Toxic even.

Dad writes his brother's eulogy while he builds a deck, uses the same stocky pencil to mark 300 mil and the story from when they drove across Australia. Back in the bulldust. When they were always playing that song. They lost the windscreen on day one. Five days later they made it to Darwin. That's the photo there, look, it was in this album all these years,

look at that t-shirt,
look at those ears.
So many miles still left to drive,
so many years.

They were younger than me
They were younger than me

Do you have a smart fuel card?
Sorry mate, ah, nah,
Probably should get one ae, nah,
Not today. Cheers. Bye.

There's a Fagan Motors car dealership in Masterton. We visit once in a blue moon to get their branded number plate frames for our cars. Frames is what you call them, the plastic around the number plate. I learn this the first time I pop in by myself. A rite of passage, stuttering the request to an interrupted stand-up meeting of slick hair and tattoos.

'These better be going on a Ford.'
'Yea mate!' I squeak. They laugh, I laugh, I drop my voice and they give me the frames. One more Christmas present off the list.

In Wellington the name on my cab driver's licence is Fagan. That's his English name, he tells me, and the name of his home village in the Middle East. Itself named for a western doctor who visited once upon a time.

I got mine from Dad
Who got his from Dad
Who got his from Dad
Who got his from Mum's
first marriage.

Inheritance is like affection,
we try to hide if we grew up with it, but it's obvious.
George got Pokémon cards and living grandfathers.
Paul got a million-dollar education and hair-growth shampoo.
I got a fuse like incense, a widow's peak, and a 1997 blue Toyota Starlet.

They were younger than me
They were younger than me

Doc Drumheller has worked in award-winning groups for theatre and music and has published ten collections of poetry. His poems have been translated into more than twenty languages, and he has performed in Cuba, Lithuania, Italy, Hungary, Bulgaria, Romania, Japan, India, China, Nicaragua, the US, Mexico, El Salvador, Ecuador and widely throughout New Zealand. He lives in Oxford, where he edits and publishes the literary journal *Catalyst*. His latest collection is *Drinking With Li Bai: 100 Haiku from China and India* (Cold Hub Press, 2022).

This poem was first published in *Landfall* 226, Heaven and Hell issue (2013).

The Second Coming
for Ben Brown

The Māori Jesus used to be my next-door neighbour
until the church in the front yard fell down.

He moved up north to be with his whānau
and I planted my roots in the hills like a hermit.

His poetry was unlike any psalm I've heard –
open mic stages were his sermon on the mount.

No false idols came before his beatitudes
dressed up in black leather and trademark sunglasses.

Thirteen apostles helped to spread his gospel
but they were more like ghosts of gang members.

Jake the Muss and Billy T. James dined together
at the last supper of fish and chips and tomato sauce.

When he shaved his long black hair mine grew longer
and now all the young dudes call me Jesus as well.

Ben Brown (Ngāti Mahuta, Ngāti Koroki, Ngāti Paoa) is an award-winning children's author, nonfiction writer, poet and performer. He was appointed inaugural Te Awhi Rito New Zealand Reading Ambassador for children in 2021. Ben writes for his supper, reads for the love of it and talks about pretty much anything if you let him. He's also a father of two, which he regards as his best work to date.

A silent poem

Dad is a silent poem
Mum is a storm
in a teacup

Love is the pause
between the lightning
strike
and the thunder
clap

Violent and warm
no cause for alarm
the harm was done

before the hand was raised
and made a wasted fist
that missed the mark

You cannot hurt the child
that does not know the
name of pain

Go on
try again and he
will show you
how the arc

of every story has no end
if you pretend
that nothing
happens

Because
of course

It
never
did

Marcus Mackenzie is a performance poet born and raised in Tāmaki Makaurau. He has competed at the NZ National Poetry Slam finals twice, once placing fourth, and has been published in *The Agenda*. His work is varied but he has a proclivity for all things rainbow and is a sucker for finding meaning in the little things.

A Letter To My Younger Self

Hey,   kid.

You are the most handsome boy at that all-girls school
thirteen years young
pimples to the Gods
lion heart
            baby face
                        so deep in the closet it looks more
                        like a home now

breathe

let them believe you are a lesbian
for as long as you need
it is okay   to allow yourself   time

you are not wasting your life by waiting
to arrive at your future
Sometimes all you can do is hold on
                                                that's okay

Your life did not start the day you
            found your name
                        got your first shot
                                    first called yourself boy

Your life started when your parents dreamed you in an ocean
and it might not have been perfect
but those early storms are what made you so strong

Your life is more than the destination
this journey is what made you / us

I know you don't love yourself yet

dream of a world with you in it
call it nightmare

Darling Boy

One day you're gonna get there
this dream
this never-ending possibility of a life
this future where the world makes space for you
and all you will want is
more

you haven't skinned enough knees yet
grown into your bones
had your heart reach out of your chest
or had someone else reach in

you don't even know what's coming
wait till the wave hits you
a freight train ready to take you to new worlds

you're gonna find the flagpole on the moon and pluck it down
slip it into your spine, so
you stand a little straighter

swim through a wave
swallow a conch shell, so
you speak a little louder

this life will never be perfect
will never not hurt sometimes
you will almost always have to fight to be understood
this life will be hard

but it will be yours
and it will be beautiful

you have always been beautiful
always been Boy
don't let anyone convince you otherwise
tell your demons
one day we will love them away

Boy
you are not a discarded box of our history burned
though I grew
I did not grow out of you
only realised how much I love you
how thankful I am for all you endured
so grateful I never left you behind like you wanted

You,
buck tooth wild-eyed Ocean
Boy
chasing your tail to catch a glimpse of the man you want to be
Boy

keep running
keep living

Boy,
you are
always kind
always angry

you will grow out of that

Boy
you are the seed planted in a plain
you're gonna grow
Boy
one day,
a question you have been waiting for all your life

Boy
they will call out your name
and you will answer

a man.

Matilda Clack is a poet currently residing in Tāmaki Makaurau. A Word Up! runner-up and WORD – The Front Line finalist in her final year of high school in 2019, Matilda has been involved in coaching, facilitating and performing poetry ever since. She is a two-time JAFA Regional Finalist and Trans-Tasman Poetry Slam champion.

tomatoes on graves

my childhood best friend is reborn by my side in a lecture theatre one Tuesday morning,
emerging from familiar flesh a newborn stranger

we ask each other questions as if a past life is nothing short of small talk to pass time;
as if we didn't just die and resuscitate with our reunion;
everyone says university is the perfect place to find new friends,
but they never warn you about old ones who'll find you,
like a haunting

she asked me questions about myself based on our bittersweet foreword
and I found out that her dog, Jack, who we both grew up with as kids,
had passed in January just a few months earlier –
she told me a story about how they had buried him in the garden,
and now a tomato plant they didn't sow there has grown on his grave

that same summer, in January, around the time Jack died,
I met somebody who was partly potential but almost everything,
who came to nothing,
who my friends think I should've held onto tighter
but I had one hand holding myself and the other realism
I still think of her sometimes,
and see her like a half-erased sketch in the margins of others I meet

with this I realised ghosts are everywhere among us;
that even our living bodies hold the dead and long-gone iterations of people we once loved
who are living in the same bodies as their new selves,
unfamiliar to us

I don't believe in the right person, wrong time, but right person, wrong reason
they were always the right people,
just not for the reasons I wished for

one day, I wave at this summer someone across campus and in the movement of my hand
I let something go
and see tiny brown seeds scattering through the air,
the next day, I am passing a worksheet across in the lecture to my childhood best friend,
and in between the pages lentils of grubby seed find root under nailbeds,
attach to the places of her personality I never got the chance to learn of

we didn't plant it there, but a strangeness has grown in the places of each other we outgrew,
a new life grown from the decay of the last we had together,
a new friendship grown from the death of our old one
a tomato grown on a grave
our time together may just be a vine wilting but this is the lifespan of tomatoes:
a short sweetness for a season and at the end, life and love
is all just
tomatoes on graves,
tomatoes on graves,
tomatoes on graves

Joy Holley lives in Wellington, and completed her Masters in Creative Writing at the International Institute of Modern Letters at Te Herenga Waka Victoria University of Wellington in 2020. Her work has been published in numerous journals including *Starling*, *The Pantograph Punch* and *Stasis*. She was one of the original performers in *Show Ponies*, a poetry performance created by Freya Daly Sadgrove. Joy's first short story collection, *Dream Girl*, was published in 2023 by Te Herenga Waka University Press.

I'M JOY HOLLEY AND I GET WHAT I WANT

. . . or i did, until now.
i am dizzy with wanting
and constantly waiting
for a sign or, more specifically,
a text. i get so attuned
to that double buzz
because you are the only person i know
who prefers texting to messenger.
i get so disappointed
when it's from a phone company instead.
i think it's hot how you're a gemini
and i'm not supposed to want you
because i'm a virgo . . . it's like, forbidden love.
it's like, everything i have ever wanted.
you're like, i am bad at letting myself have what i want
and i'm like, i can't relate.
you tell me that your grandmother has always told you
'you can have anything you want,
you can't have everything.'
i tell you, 'actually you *can* have everything.'
you disagree. i want to give you everything
you want, and also teach you how
to give yourself what you want,
which is quite virgo of me. i truly believe i am perfect
for you and that we would be a disaster.
i could prove to you that love is more
than just a chemical reaction and you
could prove to me that it isn't, if you wanted to,
but i get the feeling you don't even know what you want.
it's not my fault that i'm an earth sign and you're all
up in the air. it's not my fault that i'm so on fire and you're so
shuffling sideways. it's not your fault either, i suppose.
once, you told me you think it's 'more mature'
to live in your fears than to live in your fantasies
and I nearly spat out my drink. more than once,
i have stayed up all night, lying in bed thinking about you.

i even got out in nature for you, i even cut my nails.
what else am i supposed to do???
i used to wish for sensible things, like getting a book published
or a flat with an attic bedroom, but now when it hits 11:11
i'm only ever wishing for you. now, i sing and dance up the street
begging the moon to make you love me
please, please! now, i get down on my knees
and pray to all my virgin mary figurines
love me bitch love me bitch love me bitch
now, i sit around all day like,
who do i have to stab around here
to get what i want?

Freya Daly Sadgrove is a Pākehā writer and performer born in Te Whanganui-a-Tara, currently living on Gadigal Country in Sydney, NSW. She is the engine behind live poetry event *Show Ponies*, whose euphoric inception was described by Motif Poetry as 'a watershed moment for poetry in performance in Wellington'. It continues to perform to sold-out crowds throughout Aotearoa and beyond. Freya premiered her poetry-rock show *Whole New Woman* as part of NZ Fringe 2023.

This poem was first published in Freya's debut poetry collection, *Head Girl* (Victoria University Press, 2020).

I DON'T CARE WHO YOU ARE WHERE YOU'RE FROM WHAT YOU DID AS LONG AS YOU LOVE ME

I WANT TO LOVE AND BE LOVED BY THOUSANDS OF MEN I WANT TO BE THE UNYIELDING INDESCRIBABLE OBJECT OF DESIRE I DON'T THINK ENOUGH PEOPLE KNOW HOW BEAUTIFUL I AM NAKED I WAS TRYING TO KEEP TRACK BUT I LOST MY DIARY I LOST IT IN FEBRUARY MUM TOLD ME SHE SOMETIMES WONDERS WHAT SHE DID WRONG WHEN WE WERE LITTLE SHE ALSO PLEADED WITH ME NOT TO INDULGE IN TOO MUCH PROMISCUOUS BEHAVIOUR BUT I IGNORED HER BECAUSE I WISH TO BE WORSHIPPED I WISH TO BE AN INFLUENCE I WISH TO BE IMMORTALISED IN MANY FORMS AND TO WITNESS THE RISE AND FALL OF THOSE FORMS WITHIN MY LIFETIME I WISH TO BE ETERNAL WHILE I AM AWAKE

MAYBE IF YOU'D KNOWN ME WHEN I WAS A TEENAGER I WOULD HAVE MADE YOU SHIFT IN YOUR SEAT THINKING ABOUT MY NEW BODY MY NEW THOUGHTS MY NEW SEX BODY MY SOFT SKIN MY THIN LIMBS PERHAPS YOUR EYELIDS WOULD HAVE FLICKERED IMAGINING THE RUSTLE OF MY UNIFORM SKIRT SUCH HEAVY PRACTICAL FABRIC SUCH AN UNBELIEVABLE EVENT TO FEEL A BOY'S HAND SLIDE UP MY THIGH TO MAKE MY UNSUSPECTING PELVIS HEAT UP OH WHAT A FINE THING IS A BOY

YES BOYS ARE SO SWEET AND SO AM I OH BOY I'M A DREAM AND NANA SAYS MY DIMPLE IS VERY PRONOUNCED I AM SKIPPING FOR BOYS I AM SKIPPING FOR BOYS I AM DANCING LIKE SOMEONE WHO IS PAID TO DANCE FOR BOYS I AM TRIPPING OVER IN FRONT OF THEM I AM BITING MY TONGUE I AM LIFTING UP MY DRESS I AM BEGGING THE BOYS TO LET ME COME NEAR I AM KISSING THE BOYS I AM KISSING THE BOYS THEY ARE KISSING MY BREASTS THEY ARE KISSING MY BELLY I AM SINKING THROUGH THE MATTRESS I AM SIGHING I CAN BE HEARD THROUGH WALLS YEAH BABY OH BABY COS I LOVE TO GET HEARD

Liz Breslin is part of various stage/page poem communities in Aotearoa New Zealand and co-founded Poetic Justice Wānaka with Laura Williamson in about 2006. Thanks to the many poets who came to perform and workshop, and host them on tour, found writing and performing opportunities beyond their own rural bubble. Liz has published two poetry collections, *In Bed with the Feminists* (Dead Bird Books, 2021), winner of the 2020 Kathleen Grattan Poetry Award for a sequence of poems, and *Alzheimer's and a Spoon* (Otago University Press, 2017).

This poem was first published in *In Bed with the Feminists*.

Spin cycle

1
It's a drying day.
I know, I've checked my phone.
Also, you can tell by looking outside.
The toetoe are rearing their plumes
against a flawless sky.
A whitewash before coffee
can help reduce mental load.

2
There is no Normal. Choose
Allergy Plus, Sportswear, Mixed Load, Super Fifteen
Cottons, Cottons Stains, Cottons Eco, Delicate/Silk
Easy Care, Dark Load, Freshen Up/Rinse
Wool, Drain, Gentle Spin, Spin.

3
The internet says the first
mechanical washing machine
            was/was not
called Thor which
            does/does not
make me think of Chris
Hemsworth and his mighty
Mjolnir in that scene
he gentle spins and I
            am/am not
spending precious Easy Care
minutes verifying this, squat
in front of the front loader. I
            feel/feel not
invisible, fortressed in this room.

4
All it takes is one
blue running sock running blue
to ruin the lot.

5
There's a trick to it, separating loads.
Pay attention to the particular
energy of garments. Thank them for their
place in your life. Love them and kiss them good
and proper bye. Fucking blue fucking socks
fucking darkloading the fresh of actual
fucking pieces I tried so hard to clean.
Fuck you and your blue, blue bleed. At the end
of the – who am I kidding? There is no
end to this mountain of spin. We're busy,
so busy, fulfilling the prophecy. One
load comes out, another goes in. One load
comes out, another goes in. The toetoe
reach Mach speed. It's going to rain.

Laura Borrowdale is a writer and educator from Ōtautahi. She has often performed at festivals such as Verb Wellington and WORD Christchurch and her work has been published in *Landfall*, *The Spinoff*, *Turbine | Kapohau* and *Reading Room/Newsroom*. She is founding editor of *Aotearotica*, a literary journal exploring intersectional feminist ideas about sexuality and gender, and her first collection of short stories, *Sex, with Animals*, was published in 2020 by Dead Bird Books.

This poem was first performed in a double-booked venue for the New Zealand Young Writers Festival, and was unexpected for those gathered for a sixtieth birthday celebration. It was first published in *Catalyst* 13 (2016).

Guilt

I am a bad mother. My children watch Donald Duck downstairs while, on my bed, I have stripped you bare. I run my tongue over your body as though you are my oasis in the desert, as though I am searching for the secret well of you.

I find the places that make you gasp, your head lifting from the pillow, your eyes half closed. You fill out my mouth, and I calculate the minutes I have left, the length of Donald's quack. The time shimmers like a mirage, and, like a bad mother, I give in.

The bedclothes shift like drifts of sand, banking up around my knees, and the salt at the back of my throat is both pleasure and pain, love and guilt. Beneath us, the children laugh and laugh.

Steph Julian (Ngāti Porou ki Harataunga) was born and raised in Taranaki, is a proud mum of two girls and is married to Lars. Steph is an accomplished public speaker and loves to use humour and surprise tactics to keep her audiences on their toes. In addition to having her poetry featured in various journals, she has had short stories published in *Huia Short Stories 14* (Huia, 2021) and *FUA Anthology* (Tatou Publishing, forthcoming). She has also recently finished writing a junior fiction novel and is currently writing a historical fiction novel for adults.

Turn About

I wake up in the shell of you,
sheets changed, of course,
as per the agreement,
but the gully of your imprint remains
in the mattress.
Your pillow, ours now,
shaped to mould your skull as you sleep.

It is my week again,
in what I'd thought was a good idea,
the apartment we pass between us like a silent baton,
swapping between parenting, our home,
and echoes of each other in these rooms.

Your toothbrush is here,
makes sense really,
but hurts me still,
your fibres and flakes on the most intimate surfaces,
inside and out of me.

I hunt for the scent of another,
or is the apartment more sacred
than vows?

I sleep in your exhalations
and smoothed surfaces.
Sheets holding secrets like knives.

Lily Holloway is screaming in a Four Square carpark. Their recent work has been published in *Peach Mag, Cordite* and *Ōrongohau | Best New Zealand Poems*. Lily is currently undertaking an MFA in Creative Writing at Syracuse University in New York.

This was the first poem Lily performed at an open mic.

you are my night terror i hope i am yours

open my mouth and sand spills out in towers and slipping hills endless
open my mouth and vomit is shot at speed chunks of green monopoly
houses marbles clumps of drain hair and pineapple lumps open my
mouth and i scream magpies robbing mutton sobbing and gasping who
go for eyes pimples scabs making meaty nests open my mouth and i
turn inside out filling bathtubs with puddles of mouthwash and sperm
cilia grasping out motherless open my mouth and i'll bite your tongue
off with my judge judy teeth and swallow open my mouth and i bleed
uterus lining through my trousers and it's got teeth in it gunky pva
blood and pubes open my mouth and i'll give you a terminal illness
with slug intestines full of rat lungworm popping and you'll run
shrieking kettle open my mouth and i'll tell you of metallic streetlights
cervical scrapings scraped knees and ego death open my mouth and my
uvula is snakes and i'm on the temple floor spilling open mosaic open
my mouth and i'll feed you translucent opal larvae that do nothing but
stare open my mouth and out tumble severed ears and none of them
match haemorrhoids fibroids and cysts cascading like old-school candies
open my mouth and out spurts piss and scalding hot coffee open my
mouth and hear dido swinging by her neck in the throne room open
my mouth and your head is a cyst and i'm multitasking driving the
northern express committing hit and runs on the harbour bridge open
my mouth and grip hangnail with teeth ripping it up to the elbow open
my mouth and i'll whisper you ate the twin in the womb slapping you
into torn stockings under freight truck wheels open my mouth and
watch me floss until i slip and hit skull keep flossing my face a bone
carving open my mouth and i know your porn of choice a gif of taylor
swift tripping in heels open my mouth and your veins are throbbing
crimson clotting and you desperately screech in pak'nsave air only siren
moons blot in and out of eyesight and we're watching we're all fucking
watching blood thickening in you hissing shoppers staring blank-eyed
over stopped trolleys convulsions and bare concrete floor.

Ila Selwyn was an MC at Poetry Live for four years and ran seven National Poetry Day events from 2007–2013 in Lopdell House, Titirangi. She also ran a monthly cabaret called Rhythm & Verse in the same venue until the building was closed for earthquake restructuring. In 2015, Ila won the Going West Poetry Slam. She has published three poetry collections, *two sisters* (Ventifact Press, 2011), *dancing with dragons* (Westridge Publishing, 2018) and *slipping between* (Masque Media, 2022).

my daughter cringes

step out in my second-hand red mini
black mesh-net tights balance
on Louie's silver platforms
his gorgeous wild heels
make my legs long and lean
a wild black wig
with a red hibiscus stuck on top
tops me off

whip in hand and
chain over shoulder
break all the slam rules
no costume, no props, no song
but what the heck
it's fun and leads to running
a national poetry day at Lopdell House
in the main art gallery where

my daughter cringes

mince my way through the crowd
chain slung over shoulder
whip in hand
grab the mic
the three improv guys play it up
follow words, movements
we laugh, the audience
(well most of them)
laughs, cheers

my daughter cringes

in the late '60s and early '70s
I teach school in white mesh-net stockings
a blue-crotched-barely-bum-cover
sometimes vinyl purple home-made hot-pants
braces, bow tie, silver boots
braless and bare feet
laugh skip and dance all the way down Queen Street
in a long slinky dress with
my daughter's best friend

my daughter cringes

now in my late 60s
approaching 70 at a far-too-rapid rate
with a wig and a role
or without
do as I please
pretend to be the queen of fuck
and suck or not
but know

my daughter cringes

because she has a mad mum
this crazy creature
her two darling little boys
love to fight over

Alina Siegfried a.k.a. Ali Jacs (she/her) is a queer spoken-word artist, author and narrative strategist from Whakatāne, with Swiss, English and Irish ancestry, currently based in Te Whanganui-a-Tara. She won the 2012 NZ National Poetry Slam and competed in the 2013 Womxn of the World Poetry Slam in Minneapolis. Alina wrote, directed and performed her solo poetry show, *Jagged Little Pilgrimage*, at the 2016 Wellington Fringe. Her first book, *A Future Untold: The Power of Story to Transform the World and Ourselves* (Systemic, 2021), is a rallying cry for humanity to solve complex systemic challenges by rewriting the narratives that underpin them.

Miss Armstrong

Her memory clearly tells her that she had a schoolgirl crush on Mr Robson,
so she can't understand why it's Miss Armstrong
she can't shake from her mind.

So she spends her days cycling around this city
avoiding all contact with boys
and wearing an oversized motorcycle helmet,
so that she doesn't have to see the reflection of her face
in the puddles of tears she has cried.

And each time she flies,
she compulsively closes her eyes that moment the plane touches down
because she believes
that in that puff of smoke, released by the fusion of rubber and tarmac,
that a miracle occurs
somewhere in the world.

And perhaps today, just maybe,
when she opens her eyes
she will suddenly and miraculously understand
other girls' fascination with guys,
and that puff of smoke will erase Miss Armstrong,
once and for all.

Because each way she turns, the enemy lurks in the night,
and through painful experience
she has gained insight
that it's not only those who are cloaked in white
who would make it their personal business to expose her.

No, see, she has discovered
that beneath the surface of many,

exists a deceptively destructive homo'faux'bia
and no, I'm not talking the obvious kind, I'm talking faux like faux fur, like,

Oh? You're a lesbian?
Oh cool. I mean, I don't care,

I-actually-have-a-cousin-who's-gay-and-he's-actually-really-cool-he's-just-like-a-regular-guy-he-talks-normal-and-everything-like-I'm-totally-okay-with-whatever-you-want-to-do-whatever-it's-fine-you-know-we-had-gay-neighbours-when-I-was-growing-up-and-we-used-to-have-them-over-for-dinner-all-the-time-I-mean-it's-not-for-me-eeeww-gross-but-hey-whatever-floats-your-boat-to-each-their-own-right??

So good for you
Good for you . . .

Good. For. You . . .

And every well-intended word flies upon misguided arrows,
manages to miss the mark entirely,
instead embedding itself firmly
into the side of a barn wall so wide
it could house all the queers in the world.

A barn wall that is stained with the blood-red letters
of all the nasty words that hover
just beneath the surface,
just behind that smoke screen of pseudo-acceptance,
and no matter the make-up of the words and the inference
the message comes through each time loud and clear, that
she.
is.
different.

So she lies awake late at night,
counting black sheep and thinking of the time
that she kissed her best friend at a party.

And how suddenly the puzzle pieces all aligned
and the sparks,
no, they did not fly
they merely pooled all around her, building up high
until up to her tightly closed eyelids
she was bathed in light.

But these days,
it's getting so bad,
that she's lost count of the times
she has stood on a rickety old platform, way up high

above a geothermal pool in her hometown,
just waiting for that soul-cleansing steam
to blow her way,
engulf her face,
and lift her high off the ground
because she figures this is the closest she will ever get
to flying through the clouds.

And she instinctively knows that the clouds don't care
whether she likes boys or girls,
because clouds are merely ghosts of the water
that flows through us all

The water that was once
a glacier-fed river
a eutrophic lake
a drop in the ocean
or just a muddy puddle of tears.

As she turns her bike for home,
she casts her eyes skyward.

Looks like it might rain.

Selina Tusitala Marsh is of Samoan, Tuvaluan, English and French descent. She was the first Pacific Islander to graduate with a PhD in English from the University of Auckland and is now a professor in the English department, specialising in Pasifika literature. Her first collection, the bestselling *Fast Talking PI* (Auckland University Press, 2009), won the NZSA Jessie Mackay Best First Book Award for Poetry in 2010. Selina represented Tuvalu at the London Olympics Poetry Parnassus event in 2012 and, as Commonwealth Poet for 2016, she composed and performed for the Queen at Westminster Abbey. Selina was New Zealand Poet Laureate 2017–2019. Her debut children's book and memoir, *Mophead: How Your Difference Makes a Difference*, was awarded Margaret Mahy Book of the Year at the 2020 New Zealand Book Awards for Children and Young Adults.

This poem was first published in *Fast Talking PI*.

Fast Talkin' PI
for Anne Waldman

I'm a fast talkin' PI
I'm a power walkin' PI
I'm a demographic, hieroglyphic fact-sheetin' PI

I'm a theorising PI
I'm a strategising PI
I'm a published in a peer reviewed journal PI

I'm a slot machine PI
I'm a lotto queen PI
I'm tote-ticket church bingo TAB PI

I'm a vegan PI
a rainbow warrior PI
I'm a protest sign against the rising waters PI

I'm a criminal PI
behind the bar graphs PI
I'm a gun smokin' patching totin' king cobra PI

I'm a fale PI
I'm a marae PI
I'm a living breathing dwelling of my ancestors PI

I'm a lazy PI
I'm a p-crazy PI
I'm a hard drinkin' hard speakin' where my eggs? PI

I'm a land-based PI
I'm a fanua PI
I'm a village is the centre of my world PI

I'm a harvesting PI
a copra sacking PI
I'm a buy tinned beef 'cos no more fish in reef PI

I'm a diabetic PI
I'm a heart-diseased PI
I'm a gout-inflated, incubated, case study PI

I'm a civa Samoa PI
I'm an ava-pouring PI
I'm a tulafale tonguing genealogy PI

I'm an independent PI
I'm a flag-raisin' PI
I'm a fa'alavelave lovin' givin' livin' PI

I'm a still PI
I'm a broken PI
I'm a wheelchair bound from drunken westie driver PI

I'm a standing PI
I'm a beehive PI
I'm a labour MP gonna be PM one day PI

I'm a quiet PI
I'm a small PI
I'm a take no lunch to school today but . . . anyway PI

I'm an all-black PI
I'm an all-white PI
I'm a gold silver bronze blue street-signed PI

I'm an angry PI
I'm a dawn-raided PI
I'm a crouching poly panther in grey lynn PI

I'm a shark-toothed PI
I'm a tatau PI
I'm a malu and a pe'a, flying fox let loose PI

I know how to be in this world
I know how to feed in its waters
I know how to read the stars and sea-birds

I know how to live off poetry
I know how to give it away

I'm a propertied PI
a self-employed PI
I'm a mocha-drinkin', horn-rimmed glasses, real TV PI

I'm a movin' PI
I'm a groovin' PI
I'm a nesian mystik stratospheric whippin' it PI

I'm a krumpin' PI
a go-for-God PI
I'm a colour-free gangsta wannabe for the Lord PI

I'm a BA PI
I'm an MA PI
I'm a PhD, BCOM, LLB, MD PI

I'm a bi PI
I'm a gay PI
I'm a cross-gendered, soul-blended, mascara'd PI

I'm a coloured PI
I'm a canvassed PI
an acrylic, oil, PVC, four by two PI

I'm a bit of both PI
a chameleon PI
a hybrid, mongrelised self-satisfied PI

I'm a shadowing PI
I'm a fathoming PI
I'm an ocean, I'm the wave, I'm the depths of it PI

I'm a territorial PI
I'm a pure blood PI
I'm a border language Stop Do Not Pass Go PI

I'm a freezing works PI
I'm an IT PI
I'm a sewing, stuffing, soaking, shaking, stirring PI

I'm a talanoa PI
I'm a ta/va PI
I'm the space, the time, the tune, the transcending PI

I'm a pair of jimmy choos
I'm a size 12 in fuchsia please
I'm a no shoe fits the foot of an earth mama

I'm a royal PI
I'm a commoner PI
I'm a coup-supported, you and you and you, deported PI

I'm a white sunday PI
an LMS PI
I'm a born-again no mandatory tithing PI

I'm tihei, that first born breath
I'm that pulsating cord
I'm that breaking water
I'm that loose knot threatening to tighten

I'm that blood clot PI
that topknot PI
that loosener of sun and skin and brothers PI

I'm a lover PI
I'm a mama PI
I'm a breast-feed till they tell you *I'm done now!* PI

I'm a Nafanua PI
I'm a warrior PI
I'm the breast-kept secret in ancient samoan warfare PI

I'm a dub dub dub PI
I'm a bebo PI
I'm a good lookin', face bookin' hookin' up PI

I'm a melting pot PI
an homogenous PI
I'm a skim milk green top fat free heterogeneous PI

I'm a denny's PI
I'm a sawadee PI
I'm a finger lickin' KFC MDs BK PI

I'm a matariki PI
I'm a slammin' poetry PI
I'm a riding high and whippin' the hide of a clydesdale PI

I'm a niu FM PI
I'm a curtained stage PI
I'm a naked and I'm laughing and cartooning PI

I'm a vaka PI
I'm a star-charting PI
I'm a navigating by nissan navara PI

I'm a long poem PI
I'm a long song PI
I'm a smooth crooner softly lullabying PI

I'm a red-lipsticked PI
I'm a big-haired PI
a multi-coloured, stilhouetted fafafine PI

I'm a crying PI
I'm a laugh too loud PI
I'm a *my jandal your mouf* derek-wannabe PI

I'm a lali
I'm where we once belonged
I'm a dream fish floating
I'm wild dogs under my skirt
I'm searching for nei nim'anoa
I'm a native daughter
I'm poètes du pacifique en couleur
I'm light in the crevice never seen
I'm the girl in the moon circle
I'm niu voices
I'm songs of love
I'm mi mere
I'm houses
I'm a pinnacle
I'm a nuanua
I'm blackstone
I'm tapa talk
I'm kakala
and langakali
and hingano
I'm tai, heart of a tree
I'm colonised people
I'm praying parents
I'm a shark-skin drum
I'm solaua, a secret embryo
I'm whetu moana
I'm a young artist in contemplation
I'm the choice of your parents
I'm an act of war
I'm na buka vivinei malivi pa zinama roviana
I'm threads of a tivaevae
I'm cyclone country

I'm a theorising slot machine
bloodless coup jimmy choos
lover blood clot melting pot
shark-toothed brothers let loose
white sunday lippy BA

I'm a fast talkin' PI

Alfred Lee has performed poetry for the past fourteen years. One of the founding poets of the spoken-word scene in his hometown of Mumbai, India, he helped set up the first paid platform for performance poetry in the city. After making New Zealand his home in 2012, he became the NZ National Poetry Slam champion in 2016. Alfred's work shines a light on contemporary issues and aims to spark positive change, one poem at a time.

Forked tongue

I understand five languages,
speak three, write in two and yet
I am not comfortable conversing
in just one dialect of English.

You see I am able to flip my tone, because
nothing makes you feel more alone than hearing
the voice you've grown listening to sound off key.

Yet what is English but an instrument our mouths were forced to play?
Way before these sounds sailed on waves,
before British tongues lashed to our shores with ships,
our mouths were equipped with movement and sound.

ष, क्ष , त्र , ज्ञ *. . . the list goes on you see for these are just some of the notes*
we were forced to forget.
Because to the English ear, this is not how dignified men spoke.
And thus dignity was now born from our throats.

In India, my home was referred to as an 'English-speaking' one.
English was reluctantly acknowledged to be my 'mother tongue' –
a term Indians use to describe their native language but
somehow that hurts more.

Because my heritage was raised by imperial surrogates.
Taught to worship a Queen, we were weaned off our native tones
so that we might learn to drone in unison.

So now when people ask me,
'You speak English so well, did you always speak it?'
I'm tempted to say, 'Of course I did. Your motherland taught me.
But I'm still a bastard
which is why she never brought me to the same table as you.
But I'm here now, and I'd like to take my seat.'

And with that I assumed victory was complete but
there were still other ways to be stopped.
I learnt I could be mocked.
My accent was made the punchline,
reducing everything I said to a joke.
'Thank you, come again' isn't just a gag. It's a refrain.
It's why sometimes my accent slips because
my tongue hurts from the strain.

Yet perhaps the biggest reason why this accent manifests,
is because I'm tired of repeating my requests.

As if you were a living embodiment of Siri
and my tone mattered more than my questions.

It's why I'm so thankful for the stage. From here, you get to gauge
if the sound of my words dull their meaning.

I hope you'll come up to me and tell me if they do but
I must warn you, I may not sound like this when we talk.

At least now, you'll know why my tongue is forked.

Tamara Tulitua was raised in Aotearoa, and flows from Sāfa'ato'a, Matā'utu, Vailima, Tanugamanono and Sapapāli'i of Samoa. An avid follower of spoken word since her youth, Tamara's debut poetry performance was in 2019. In 2021 she completed a Masters in Creative Writing at Te Pūtahi Tuhi Auaha o Te Ao (IIML) at Te Herenga Waka Victoria University of Wellington and was the 2022 Creative New Zealand Emerging Pasifika Writer in Residence at the IIML. Tamara's work has appeared in literary journals and other online publications including *The Pantograph Punch*, *Dominion Post* and *Turbine | Kapohau*. As archivist/artist/activist, she uses language as shield/sword/spade: utility defining form.

y/ours not mine

savalivali mai ia
lou mata fiafia
lupe o le manu e
luelue malie
savalivali mai ia
lou mata fiafia
lupe o le manu e
luelue malie

e iloa le tamaitai Samoa i lana tu ma lana savali
tu
ma
savali

savalivali means go for a walk
tautalatala means too much talk
alofa ia te oe means I love you
take it easy fai fai lemu

you are not your own
we are our own
we are ours not theirs
they are other
never become other/never become theirs

your words are our words
unending passive sentence
border crossing to active terrain
we are object and subject
weakened voice in rugged plains

we are speaking with your forked tongue
unknotting itself, prostrate
disciple of the sentence
prayer beads through verbs
you perform at the altar

who told you
to be a noun
is to be known
a being all your own?

lau lupe ua lelo
lele I le vao mao
talofa e lau pele
lau pele ua leiloa

the view of the Empire from the va'a, is splendid
it looks so beautiful, doesn't it, son?
the people inside must want for nothing
they don't get up before the sun
find ways to numb the nagging pulse in their brain that
the boredom along an assembly line will threaten to
drag their sanity down the chain,
through that sortor and into a cereal box, a can, a Ralta appliance, a box of prime cuts, a jam jar, a Wattie's can, a passenger's suitcase, a hotel drawer, a commercial cleaning vacuum bag, a bus engine, a fast-food vat, a sealed road, a shipping container, a tunnel of shit my father is cleaning

pese ma le fiafia
pese ma faafetai
pese ma le loto
ia leo tele ai

if you learn their words
if you learn their sounds
if you learn
learn
learn
but never speak unless spoken to you will
rise
rise
rise

you will be high in the Empire like those people
see them not needing anything
talk like them and walk like them but
do not become them
you must walk like a Samoan Girl
Good Samoan Girl knows how to talk and how to walk
our dove
flower in our ear
seraphic life on the mantel
slicked back bun with eyes on the floor

le masina ua vaai i luga o mauga
mafaufauga e le uma
le masina ua vaai i luga o mauga
mafaufauga e le uma

Michelle Bolton was a writer, performer and mental health advocate who championed the growth and support of performance poetry in Aotearoa New Zealand. A co-founder and driving force of the NZ National Poetry Slam, she hosted at Poetry Live, MC'd LIVE at the Library Bar and coordinated the Going West Poetry Slam. In addition to creating stages for other poets, she performed with The Literatti, toured Melbourne in 2012, completed a Bachelor of Creative Writing at Manukau Institute of Technology and published her own books. Her impact and legacy is alive and thriving in Aotearoa's poetry scene and she is missed.

Pieces I – Just. Listen. To. Me.

It would be cool to be more obviously painted
on the outside, on the skin side,
the side seen as most closely acquainted;
so it would take no more than an ear-cocked firm grip
on recognition's reins to slow down its carriage
to 'now you're speakin' my language!'

Be great to be available in HD
when I explain why I wish for these
mount'd merits in the halls of minority's fame –
why I wish to lay claim to suffrage's lonely flame . . .

Just. Listen. To. Me.

Whether you hear me twang and clack
like a cheese grater down your back;
or maybe you're taken aback
by my accent's euphoric attack
no matter how you pick up my slack! –

you have to agree
there's an eyesore of a difference
between you all and me,
and it isn't as easy a difference
for you to see the way I see.

You see you just may well be
looking at THE one and only
Anglo-Canadian–Spanish (ai mami)-
Yankee-Fucken-California-Doodle-Dandee-
Southern-Belle-Give 'em Hell-
Wellingtonian-Empire-State-
East-Coast-Jaffa-Coasted-
Proud-Ass Kiwi

that might ever be
So why do I claim all these pieces?
For the same reason they've made me all I'll ever be –
and that's proud of every aspect of my genealogy,
a Canadian babe, to a pair of expat Kiwis,
born in time to leave my birthplace estranged from me.
You see Español was my first native tongue,
mi casa as bilingual as they come.
My folks had mainly English words alone –
far removed from the palabras de la comunidad española.
The way in which yo entiendo, and the manner in which yo he oido
was mirror'd in how yo hablé to the personas of my home.

I was becoming this discontent'd mezcla –
a maravillosa hybrid resounding
through inocente's misunderstanding
peppering more piezas in me
with the pride I pass on from ahi.

Mexico, I can say honestly
yo respeto esa parte de mi
and I'm sorry for suppressing so deeply
the pieces you gave me so freely
but I was a mere inexperto baby
when mi familia and the pieces forming in me
again made it time to leave my country.

When American began to mezclar in me
the jigsaw of my personified dignity
they overlapped its edges in English conformity,
and shamed mi Español's spontaneity
to burrowing so deep it went past gravity

But the true impact on my reality
is the piezas de fuego they left
burning in me.

Muchas Gracias, mi primera casa, and much respect I bestow.
Mucho Gusto par alas piezas de magnifico Mexico!

Only wish I could wear it like a badge aquí
on the outside, on the skin side so you all can see
I can empathise with the tides of cultural rarity,
cast adrift on the waves of a pretty lonely sea;
caught between a land I won't swim to
and an island that won't swim to me.

Ryan Gordon Teura a.k.a. Lazy Eye is an artist who has spent the past decade honing his craft through making music, performing spoken-word poetry and engaging in acappella rap battles throughout New Zealand. Ryan's love of writing incorporates his witty humour, intricate lyricism and a passion for all things Kiwi. He placed third in the Open Entry category of the E Tū Whānau Spoken Word Competition in 2021.

Men's Mental Health

To my brothers who are down and out, I'm here to help
so let's have a kōrero about men's mental health:
now us tāne are quite sensitive but won't confess it
we treat our fears like anonymous letters, we don't address it
Depression among Kiwi males can lead to dire straits
and when it comes to suicide we have one of the higher rates
It's heartbreaking how we've set this bar
so it's on us to confront how we let it get this far
See life gives us obstacles that we're forced to partake
    relationship break-ups that lead to heartbreak
    loneliness kicks in waves of anxiety
    feeling left out like you have no place in society
    unemployed yet finances are badly in need
When you're the man of the house with a family to feed
    comparing your imagery to others in better shape physically
    suffering a permanent injury or having a disability
    diagnosed with an illness that's mentally
    or abused verbally, physically, sexually
I speak on behalf of those bros who can relate
like pāua at the beach there's only so much a man can take
Now do I cry at times? Hell yeah
I don't care I'll share it out there because it's beneficial to my welfare
Now there's a stigma that we're supposed to harden up but it doesn't always work like this
you see the path to peace is a journey not a light switch
however better days will come and this is a fact
you see it's not how we fall but how we find our way back
Don't keep things bottled up reach out
speak out and there's no shame in anyone who needs help
there's no harm in therapy or seeing a counsellor
they could help add things up like algebra
or if you're too whakamā for a stranger to talk to
link up with whānau and friends to support you

Surround yourself with positive company
and anyone at any time can always come to me
see I'd much rather you hit me up at early hours in the morning
than turn up to your tangi and everyone's mourning
I'll keep it a hundred this is straight from the heart
if you don't shine a light on something it'll remain in the dark
now although life can seem like a never-ending struggle
I promise there's a light at the end of every tunnel

Ricky Day was born in Te Matau-a-Māui, fled for greener pastures and then humbly found his way back. He can now be heard performing poems about life, death and rabbits at the monthly Common Poet's Society at the Common Room in Hastings, and has taken the stage at both the Fringe in the 'Stings and Hawke's Bay Readers and Writers festivals.

Snuggly Bunny is Missing

Snuggly Bunny is missing.

No four words could strike a greater terror in my heart.

Snuggly. Bunny. Is. Missing.

All else must cease once those words have been spoken. Put down your tea, your popular magazine, your snatched moment of peace. Heed the call, round up the posse, for tonight, we ride! We ride, and we must not rest until that brown ball of synthetic fluff has been returned to the most grateful of tiny hands.

Upturn everything. Rifle through all the drawers. Toss the room like you're searching for the microfiched plans of a secret superweapon, but please bear in mind that Snuggly Bunny is much, much more important than the microfiched plans of a secret superweapon, so undertake your room tossing with additional vigour.

Stop at nothing. The bunny must be found.

Once, he spent six hours trapped in a locked box emblazoned with unicorn stickers. Six hours of tears and recriminations until a miracle guess released the combination, clunk-click, and he was free! I thrust him aloft to the light in triumph, like a miner returned from the brink of an international catastrophe, a boy plucked from the mouth of a swollen storm drain.

Put me in the papers, I'm a goddamn hero.

One day, my daughter – *very* serious – shows me all the places where time and too much care have worn away at Snuggly's fur, leaving him bare. She calls these patches 'love spots'.

I swing her up into my arms and tell her I, too, had love spots, once, on a toy I left behind long ago. But I fudge that last part, and she mishears me. Weeks later I see her looking me up and down.

Dad? She says. Where are your love spots?

One day
she will put Snuggly down
and never pick him up again.

One day
I will put her down
and I will never pick her up
again.

Look me over closely. Take your time.
Can you see where the fur has worn away?

Tim Heath writes poetry and, occasionally, gets it published. He was MC at Poetry Live for several years and has won poetry slams in New Zealand and Australia including Poetry Idol, WOMAD, Going West, Burnie Gold Cup (Tasmania) and Bellingen (rural NSW). Tim has published a poetry collection, *Not as the Crow Flies* (Graduate Press, 2018), and a memoir, *The Accidental Teacher* (Allen & Unwin, 2021). He writes about everyday life and believes poetry should be straightforward, even funny. Tim's time for writing is happily compromised by 9.6 grandchildren, reading, cooking, gardening, golf, ocean sailing, sports, tending an ageing Grey Lynn villa . . . and dreaming.

The Sunshine of my Youth

They tell me there is a melanoma in my back.
I don't believe it is a melanoma –
I think it is a nasty little octopus
with sun-fuelled and ambitious
tentacles that burrow below the surface
and prepare for a deep-sea dive.

I like pets, have always had a dog,
but I have no love for my little octopus.
I do not wish to feed it,
to be responsible for it
or show it to my friends.

I do not wish to watch it grow.

Young people, clever and beautiful,
have tried to dig it out
with sharp, precise instruments.
They are kind and skilful.
They talk to me, laugh
at my cheery conversation,
not because it is amusing,
more because it says I'm an old stoic,
trained not to be any bother.

Soon, they will start a third octopus hunt.
Soon, I will lose myself
in their back-to-front gown,
put on the silly hat,
place control and identity
in an untidy pile with my clothes.

I want to instruct them:
'Take a sharp bloody teaspoon
and just scoop the bastard out.'

But I don't.
And they don't.

I am lucky.
I am not suffering.
I am not a prisoner
listening for the footsteps
of the men who want
to extract the last of my knowledge.

I am not a helpless sea creature,
tentacle entwined and dragged
towards a beaky mouth.

I am just an aging man
who wants to spend lots more time
in his garden.

John Allison has published six books of poetry and his poems appear regularly in magazines. He is a frequent performer of his poetry in and around Christchurch. His poem-sequence 'Poetics of Water' was set to music by Pieta Hextall for voice and chamber ensemble and performed in 2021. Of 'Ode to the Chez Eelco' he writes: 'Ah, to be 18 in 1968 . . . ! We were Bohemian, we were Beat and suddenly Hippies were popping up like mushrooms. Some of us remember being there. The Chez Eelco in Nelson's Trafalgar Street was perhaps New Zealand's first European-style café.'

Ode to the Chez Eelco

for Eelco Boswijk, 1929–2013

I was born there
learned what chess was
learned that jazz was
learned how coffee's meant to be
learned what friendship can become
it was the summer late in '68 so we talked of
MLK & RFK / Paris / Prague / Chicago / Vietnam
with Sartre & Camus getting a look in / Kafka too
(not just because there were copper cockroaches on the walls)
& we talked about the Revolution & then
did our homework & went back to school on Monday
to benefit from English history / English poetry
meanwhile James K. Baxter heard the call to go to Jerusalem
Allen Ginsberg howled into the night & on the road
the other JK bummed dharma with Gary Snyder
(I read Richard Brautigan & fished for trout on the Motueka)

We all witnessed the tidal surge of youth in those
fervid early evenings every Friday & Saturday / then
the emptying out into the streets / cars / parties / back seat
sex any way anywhere up the Maitai
or else lying in the dunes at Tahunanui Beach
leaping bonfires on the Waimea River bed or out at Atawhai
returning towards midnight to tell the tales
the tidal basin of desire suddenly brim-full once more
the moon riding high & so were we
& Eelco moved among us so urbane & suave
saying 'buy coffee or go' & so we bought coffee & did not go

This year of mine was the miracle of *Music from Big Pink*
when 'Suzanne' took me down to her place
near the river & *The Hangman's Beautiful Daughter*
soared into *Astral Weeks* while the masses argued

about The Beatles & The Rolling Stones
('Hey Jude!' / 'The time is right for fighting in the street, boy' . . .)
though in the shadows there was talk of the new
CBS LP of the *Goldberg Variations* played by Glenn Gould
or of *Miles in the Sky* (with diamonds) / 'The Girl
from Ipanema' sung by Astrud Gilberto & my friend
loved her for the sound of her voice but Oh I loved her for
the sound of her name & then my friend
said 'Try this' & it was The Velvet Underground
White Light/White Heat & then he said 'Try this' & it was
a joint & holy shit that was something
else on Nelson's Cathedral steps on a hot summer's midnight

Walking back into the caff I was born right then

Before that I had watched myself moving in the world as if
far off in the distance / a marionette dangling from
tangled strings I had no way of handling
all my songs stuck in my gullet but
that summer I came down into my life & loves
& slipped into my body as a hand into a glove-puppet

& so became my own story & so began my telling

Clémence Williams (she/they) is a WORD – The Front Line alumnus and Word Up! winner. Currently living in Te Whanganui-a-Tara, she is a passionate biology student and frequenter of Windswept slams. Clémence was in the winning team of the 2022 Wellington team slam. They have also performed at the Wellington Feminist Creative Community poetry night and the Comedy vs Poetry Face/off. For Clémence, life is weird and wonderful and she hopes to write many more poems about it.

I Love You to Courtney Place and Back

We're running wild through the veins of the city
Stumbling cross-legged haze
Spinning round street poles
Slurring I love yous,
beckoned by the lampposts in the distance like moths to a flame.

Us women that show their teeth and bite when told to smile,
us goddesses (and mild public disturbances at the worst of times).
Our arms will be wrapped so tightly from purse to girlfriends
we'll develop collective rigor mortis,
(it's sexier than it sounds and we wear it well).
We'll call ourselves untouchable,
invincible,
if just for one evening.

The toilet stall neighbours will join you eventually
and at 3 a.m. you'll write them into your will,
for how can you be strangers on a night like this?
Even if their names slip your grasp by sunrise,
you can find them somewhere out there
on a suspiciously sticky floor,
waiting to compliment your hair and warn you not to text your ex.

Girls on a night out are magnetic.
Getting pushed about in the masses
but reuniting if it's the last thing we do,
echolocate our way back if we must,
then take the long walk home
hand in hand, passing fries like a drunken communion,
Stumbling
Spinning
Slurring . . .

Get home safe
Text me when you're there
I love you
I Love You
I Love You

. . . and we really do.

Cassandra Barnott (Raukawa, Ngāti Huri) is a writer across worlds, language unlearner, avid weeder, reo dreamer. In 2021 she published her chapbook with accompanying audio work *How | Hao* (The chronicle of <_____>). Her performance highlights include reading from *How | Hao* in two voices at Brisbane Writers Festival in 2022, performing with roots-funk band The Locals at Paekākāriki Town Hall in 2020 and sharing off-limits words underground at the offline, invite-only Night of Untold Stories in Porirua in 2019. Cassandra's poetry has been published in *No Other Place to Stand: An Anthology of Climate Change Poetry from Aotearoa New Zealand* (Auckland University Press, 2022) and *Black Marks on the White Page* (Penguin, 2017), and in literary journals *Cordite*, *Brief*, *Ora Nui*, *Tupuranga*, *Te Whē ki Tukorehe* and *Landfall*.

don't mess with my pāraerae

these are my magic slippers || they're no jawbone but they'll do
papatūānuku's sucking || wants to dirty me up
disturb my rongo with some tū || but i'm safe

the silicon envelope between || these soles &
her flattened grass blades || is infinite

an asymptote || a paradox of xeno || an information autobahn || for amoebal drifters
a fibre-optic whāriki || threaded || with speeds & directions more intricate || than the inter-iwi politics of mycorrhizae

can you see it? || the length i'll ride || escaping depth?

watch me pad out || to the rotary line || peg our wash & bite the rust || accruing round its pole
pad up || to the raised bed || pluck parsley by the fist || pad back

duck in under the kūaha || cross fingers
got my ancestors on side || wipe slippers on the mat

watch me || circumnavigate this world || te ao mārama entire
from fizzing garden || to dusty halls & stages || to urupā of far-flung tūpuna

wherever i go i surf || walk on water || glide
i'm marty mcfly & || my slippers stay dry

oh they know || they catch the gossip || could snitch on the makawe || in the kīhini
but they demur || my good lil kaitiaki || nothing sticks || to my tikanga freezers || i believe
they'd skate the belljar of the earth || to save me

so lucky to wear these slippers || & free bonus magic dishcloth || magic tea towel
magic hairbrush || magic kai that's no longer kai || when it's a bedroom snack

so lucky to pay no mind || to what goes on || beyond profane space || lucky to have ancestors
who don't keep score || just pass through || forgiving me || flying on

i admit that when i feel || tikanga ripple || through my subtle body
shady & minute || the growth rings whisper ||
in millennia to come || u may yet get unified || get skilled

at navigating || this bewitched earth sea & sky || from which u hide
pause the bluster long enough || to take the shoes off yr shame
lift the carpet & || step inside

but for now my demigod's still māui || can't whakapapa to xeno
my underfoot technologies don't index || enlightenment spirits
breaking rules is || my inheritance

& if not māui then || his younger sister || on one more trip back || to muriranga-whenua
o grandmother || protect me from my || bad decisions daily

no one stole your slippers yet || did they?

Joan

A poetry show by Carrie Rudzinski and Olivia Hall
HYSTERICAL
Tauranga 16th Ave Theatre, 30 April
Hamilton The Meteor, 5–6 May
Christchurch Little Andromeda, 12–14 May
Nelson Refinery ArtSpace, 20–21 May
Wellington BATS Theatre, 31 May – 3 June
Dunedin New Athenaeum Theatre, 17–18 June
Auckland Basement Theatre, 5–9 July
BOOK NOW at HWSPOETRY.COM

3

Re-earth your roots

Amber Esau (Ngāpuhi, Manase) is a Sā-māo-rish writer from Tāmaki Makaurau. She is a poet, storyteller, amateur astrologer and professional procrastinator. She was the 2014 Going West Poetry Slam champion. Amber's work has been published in *Puna Wai Kōrero: An Anthology of Māori Poetry in English* (Auckland University Press, 2014), in collections for young readers *Skinny Dip!* (Annual Ink, 2021) and *Annual 3* (Annual Ink, 2022), and in *The Spinoff*.

Shapeshifter

This is how we bend light:
a slipstream in the diamond
turning
angles with edges
it sharpens against itself

slowly forming and reforming
the fog from the shine
slicing
through rectangles
with the blade of a prism

shifting colours down the spine
and out its mouth
smoothing
all the ripples
into solid bands of blues and reds
and yellows.

This is how we hold sound:
the whenua's in the pātē
hollowed
slits that echo
behind the shape of a waka

skin of the mulberry
hung up in the background
scraped,
dried and beat
to a paper muslin

parting lips at the cloth
our voices strain through
the cords of a thousand throats

humming
lost words
over the rattle of wood.

This is how we make shapes:
the shadow on a wing
flies
until the ink sac loosens
and explodes

across the skin
a night that's relentless
grips
each body in embrace
and plays the strike

across the stars
a sisterhood of blood and myth
pulls
shadow from the bone
mapping the Malu onward
in fine, dark netting.

This is how we shed skins:
aitu in the memory
will peel
off like sunburn
pulling the exorcised blister
with the nail underneath
finding where it
will smooth
over raw pink
petal-covered water

bobbing in the ripples
a tender freshness
will shine
at the first strip of light
coming in through the trees.

Shapeshifting in quarter notes
until the skies boil then cool
to a pulpy jar of preserves

next to dented tins of peaches
and half-poured bags of flour
sifting and slapping the freshest meat

in between dusty coughs
the archaeology has no bones
but sound
the soft undoing
of bodily noise until it's only frequency

and shuffled steps through sand
dried leathers ground into it
shifting in and out of each other   time

and matter casting over the slick newborn
with a kind of sluggish
kina softness running down the chin
from a halved spiky shell.

This is how we build universe:
a dusting of stars
one word fixes and glows
in fine grains of gas
spindly letters poking
and prodding into the pitch

dark as a pe'a – darker even
each new word once shapeless
moves around the base of a mountain
like the awa reflects stanza
in the sky

small rooms, all windows
stars as thin as gauze
shimmer in the wind
crawling in under the glass
we stitch them until storied
and shift shapes in the echo.

Stevie Davis-Tana (Ngāpuhi, Ngāti Hine, Te Arawa, Ngāti Raukawa ki te Tonga) is a māmā and creator living in Tāmaki Makaurau. With a passion for creativity, identity and storytelling, she works as a television director and facilitator around Aotearoa. Stevie has a Masters in Human Rights and is passionate about advocating for social change in our communities. As a recent graduate of Te Pīnakitanga ki te Reo Kairangi, she is dedicated to championing te reo Māori in all spaces that she is in.

Te Awa Atua

I bleed in rubies
Return my riches to the earth
Soak the soil in red redemption
This shedding is the embodiment of my divinity
This cycle is my sacred birthright
The pulling of the tides as I dance with the moon

Te Whare Tangata cradles the potential of the universe
The birthplace of humankind
We hold the sanctity of creation between our thighs

When the white missionary men came
They colonised our menstruation with shame
Called us dirty until we believed it
Taught our daughters how to hide in silence
That girl meant polluted instead of powerful
Policing indigenous procreation is a form of genocide
The colonisers' secret weapon

Generations later I am still finding white picket fences lodged in my womb
Every time a girl is humiliated for bleeding
Reclaiming this blood is an act of decolonising my body
I will not carry the burden of shame any longer
Keep conversations hidden in closets
Or bury my shedding out of convenience
I will glory in the sanctity of my body
That this is proof of my survival
I will teach my daughters that they do not have to whisper when they say the word period
Teach my sons how to honour the most sacred bloodshed

Hineahuone, formed from the red clay of Papatūānuku
Waiwhero flows open doors to new life
And so her divine power lives on within us
Wāhine

Birth our children from Kurawaka soil
We are descendants of mother earth
Bloodlines that run from dirt to uterus

I am the closest to Godhood when I am bleeding
This blood is baptism
This blood is political on my terms
This blood is survival

Arihia Latham is a Kāi Tahu, Kāti Mamoe and Waitaha writer and rongoā practitioner living in Te Whanganui-a-Tara. She has performed her poetry in *Ngā Oro Hou* (2021) as part of Auckland Writers Festival and at Story Collider, slam events and Poetry with Brownies. Arihia's work has been widely anthologised and her debut collection, *Birdspeak*, was published in 2023 by Anahera Press.

Tikanga in the suburbs

We stand, looking at the earth
Piles of decaying stink
Steam rising
Our tīpuna flickering
Their pūkana eyes in
The sunlight slanting
Across us as we dig
I push my hand inside the hot mound
And I am surprised at the life
That hits me again as the small body on my chest writhes

We settle the ipu
Into the hole
I am not sure I am ready to leave this
Part of us here
But I can see the look on all your faces
And so we start to push and crumble the
Whenua ki te whenua
I have pushed and crumbled
And need to be rebuilt from clay
I need the mauri to be blown into my nose
I need the ora to flood my veins
I need the part of me buried to
Disintegrate or burn
To find something of me rising again
To find something of myself again
To see my face for who it was
But the earth is under my nails
And in my eyes and smeared on my cheeks
And my babies are in it and of it and
Were in me and of me

They are sitting waiting for me to row us to the shore of
Something new and I don't know how to tell them
That the tide is out and it might not come back in
That I don't know the tikanga of these things

Or when time will turn back to shine a light on their soft cheeks
It might be moonlight and shiver moths into their hair
Beating pūrākau into their ears
That only come with te pō.
We stomp down the whenua around a small rākau and we karakia
And the words are whispered in the trees and rise from the soil
The sun is starting to set
The colour of blood
Still reminding me birth was only days ago
Yet something in me is craving the water
The purity of being washed and tapu lifted
It's not up to us to decide that though is it
It's not up to us to make up the timeline of things we don't fully understand
I can only watch you all immerse yourselves in the bodies of water that I crave
And nurse the baby till my eyes are
Making rain fall
It falls till our house has a moat
Like I am a princess that has magic
Mauri in my eyes that made me do it
I made this happen with my desire and resentment
I made the tide rise to our boat
And now I have to figure out where we are going.

Dietrich John Soakai is of Tongan, Samoan, German, English and Fijian decent. Dietrich joined the South Auckland Poets Collective (SAPC) in 2011 and has performed throughout Aotearoa including at WORD Christchurch, New Zealand Libraries Conference, Parachute Festival and Festival One. He travelled with SAPC to the Brave New Voices Slam in San Francisco and has performed at Da Poetry Lounge in Los Angeles. Other performances include an original poem with the Auckland Philharmonia Orchestra and the Adelaide Fringe with Nova Riche. Dietrich is employed by Action Education and is a founding member of WORD – The Front Line.

Skydiving

I'm gonna go skydiving,
yup, well I've heard they've got weight restrictions.
But that ain't stopping me from trying!

Too many people be wishing they could do something crazy,
so this
is me, come with me, no if buts or maybes, LET'S GO SKYDIVING

> Ah . . . no thank you, you must be OUTSIDE YO MIND!!!??

Okay,
but tell that to a young bird on its first time when it tries to fly
tell that to anyone who's done anything worth remembering, whose memory
inspires, calls us to go higher, further and faster.

I'm a go skydiving! And leave a perfectly intact aircraft, for no other reason
than because.
Because I'm sick
of the woulda, coulda, shoulda.
Because I'm sick
of weak yellow belly justification,
there will never be the right time, so why act all patient, the best part of life
is participation

> 'This ain't a good idea, why would you do such a thing? You've got too much to live
> for!!' I hear them scream.

PFFT!

I SAY – I'm a go skydiving
Coz you can stay here
in your comfortable chair
but home is suspended in the air somewhere
between safety and certainty.
See safety was my comfortability,
and the ground?
Well, that's my certainty. But THIS I'm certain of,
I would rather have tried, cried, flied, high,
than wonder why, how, and die,
having done nothing, doing nothing.

I don't wanna survive, *I wanna live!*

I wanna live with the belief on the inside of me
that I can
change the world

that love
really does exist, that life
should be approached with open hands,
not closed fists,
that the union between lovers is unbreakable when sealed with a kiss
that yes,
they'll have their challenges,
but 60 years down they'll only recall bliss,
that God willing my children will also believe this.

That if you really want to live
you must jump out of plain
your comfortable, ordinary plane,
and FALL
in this process your heart will beat at a pace that lightning dances too,
your vision will be heightened and your face may turn pale and blue,
but as you come plummeting towards certainty, you'll begin to laugh and see and FEEL
from a perspective that safety could never reveal / nor give,
it's in this moment,
between safety and certainty,
you know what it means to live.
See me?
I'm gonna go skydiving.

Miriam Barr (she/her) has been involved in performance poetry in New Zealand since the early 2000s, often working in collaboration with other poets, artists, musicians, film makers and dancers. She was the inaugural Poetry Idol slam champion in 2007, and has actively supported the wider poetry community through her time as an MC at Poetry Live, as creative director of poetry theatre collective The Literatti and as National Poetry Day coordinator. Her poetry has appeared in journals, anthologies, academic texts and art exhibitions both in New Zealand and abroad. Her first major collection, *Bullet Hole Riddle*, was published in 2014 by Steele Roberts.

This poem was previously published online at MadinAmerica.com and in the *Journal of the New Zealand College of Clinical Psychologists* 31 (2021).

Statistics for the Social Sciences

I had this idea I could join the system
and help change it from the inside
but you can't join the system
and not join the system.

You've got to put
your best foot forward
do not rock the boat
well, rock the boat a little
but not much
don't tip the boat
don't ask anyone to build a new one
do not redesign the boat
definitely don't point out
hey, the ocean isn't deep here, you know
and we could walk
if we don't mind getting our knees wet.

Do not let your knees get wet.

If your knees get wet, keep it to yourself
we don't talk about the wetness of the water here
we study the motion of the wave
the molecular structure, the parts
their correlation to the shore and the clouds
and the rain and the temperature
we do not talk about the feel of it
there are names for speaking of the feel of it
unboundaried/anecdotal/bias.

I am full of bias in a boat
of balanced, nodding quiet
swallowing my reactions back like stones.

Feelings are things we study
not things we have out in the open
we are individuals
our perspectives are invalid
your single-n sample study lacks
generalisability
see, that's just your opinion there
it only counts
when a majority agrees with you.

In statistics, one is insignificant
one has no power
one is an outlier
outliers can get trimmed off
we are afraid of being outliers
so we become swallows instead.

A crowd of silent swallows
billowing out across the sky
and our feet, our knees
are perfectly dry.

Aiga Tupulaga Poementary is intergenerational family poetry created by Reverend Papa Mua Strickson-Pua (Gafa Aiga Purcell, Malaela, Aleipata, Upolu, Samoa, Ireland, France; Aiga Pua, Papa Sataua, Savaii, Samoa; and Aiga Laiman, Canton, China) and Linda Strickson-Pua (genealogy Strickson, Peterborough, Fulham, London and Hull family, Southampton, England), grandparent poets of mokopuna poets Wilco Strickson-Pua, Jayda Pocock and Cheden Ah Yek Strickson-Pua. Aiga Strickson-Pua has published a three-Tupulaga intergenerational poementary, 'New Zealand-born dreams' (*Whanake* 4, 2018), a first for Aotearoa Niu Sila literature.

This poem was first published in 2020 as part of the Auckland War Memorial Museum project Tāmaki Poems

BUSH WALK

Two-generational Alofa Poementary dedicated to Nana Linda Strickson-Pua who has a deep love for nature and her aiga/whānau.

BUSH WALK verse #1
Toast and butter
food for our bush walk
Jayda, Che, Papa Mua, me
to Onetangi bird sanctuary
our forest needs sunshine to grow
it needs our love to grow
feeling happy being family
my story my poetry
We never walk alone . . .
[Wilco Strickson-Pua, 6 years old]

NGAHERE HĪKOI verse #2
We spray our boots
Wilco, Che, Papa Mua and me
following the Stream Walk
now chasing Che
seeing colours of light green, red moss,
yellow, brown, dead leaves, dead branches,
fluffy, rough, wet flowers, strong smells
flowing air,
smells like honey, don't hurt the bush
and respect nature
We never walk alone . . .
[Jayda Pocock, 8 years old]

VAO SAVALI verse #3
Green grass
birds and trees
all surround me.
Constant chatter about movies
and ice cream.
Papa stumbling along
while me complaining
about all that is wrong.
It's more than a walk
it is a pact.
Ever since we jumped
off the ferry onto Waiheke Island
we've never looked back.
All because our Nana Linda
she keeps us in line
we always walk together
like a pact we stay together
We never walk alone . . .
[Cheden Ah Yek Strickson-Pua, 14 years old]

AT THE BACK verse #4
I see Che leading
Jayda behind holding number two
while Wilco checks to make sure Papa's OK
these young ones are doing a trek
towards their Malaga Ola life journey
but also creating their poetry verses
growing into their futures
among the natural beauty
of our Onetangi bird sanctuary
Waiheke Island Tāmaki Makaurau
before Tāne Mahuta, Tīpuna and Atua
our Aiga Wairuatanga coming together
these Mokopuna make us very proud
Hence we never walk alone . . .
[Papa Mua Strickson-Pua, 59 years old]

Poementary:
** For God has not given us a spirit of fear, but of power and of love and of a sound mind.*
(2 Timothy 1:7 New King James Version)
**Ngahere hīkoi in te reo Maori means bush walk; vao savali in Gagana Sāmoa means bush walk.*

A writer, poet and performer based in Central Otago, **Laura Williamson** is the editor of *1964: mountain culture / aotearoa*. She is a member of The Blue Moments Project song and spoken-word cycle and wrote *The Bike and Beyond: Life on Two Wheels in Aotearoa New Zealand* (BWB Texts, 2016). Laura also features in *Rail:lines The:film* (2022), a documentary about a bike-powered poetry tour of the Otago Central Rail Trail with fellow poets Annabel Wilson and Liz Breslin.

Nothing happens in contradiction to nature, only in contradiction to what we know of it.

We found the flashlight in a cave on the Kepler Track. It's a really good flashlight.
The beam is strong and true, and when I carry it to the woodpile at night, I feel like
Dana Scully, the star of every dark room in every homicide basement of the nineties.
She was not afraid of cornfields, abandoned warehouses or the feds.

The flashlight is so bright, when you point it at a star, it's like they are two fingertips.
Light touches light. You could blind an alien with it, if you had to.

Johannes Kepler was the father [they were all fathers back then] of celestial mechanics.
He used maths to plot the paths of the planets, he saw the sky whir above us for a reason.
Stars scar the dark. Space is a vault for light.

Scully wielded her flashlight like a weapon.
She could bury you with science.
She wore pantsuits,
she found impossible things,
she was the daughter of time.

We study the past as a form of contact tracing, a way to weigh the knowledge
we are born into. All those lost children. I feel for Kepler's wives.
The experts argue, but they don't really know what light is.
When you are looking at light, you are looking at light. Light looks back and laughs.

Stars scar the path of the flashlight. *Hey Kepler, I touched a planet!* I measured the skies.

Golden Bay poet **Mark Raffills** has toured and performed throughout New Zealand at poetry groups, live venues and festivals including Waitaki and Nelson arts festivals, NZ Fringe and Poetry Live. He was a finalist in the 2011 and 2015 NZ National Poetry Slams, has self-published three books of poems, while his weekly video poems on Facebook have attracted over 110,000 views in the last five years. Raffills has coordinated both Nelson and Golden Bay Live Poets groups over the last thirty years, has collaborated with artists, musicians and poets on various projects and events and is a member of the Peace Co-Op Theatre Co.

Love as the moon is

On clear nights, the moon paints a gold path
on the sea, on the lake and on the estuary.
It can be seen from that upstairs window,
the moon,
round like love,
hovering,
making light out of the darkness,
turning trees into secret shadows
far from the breaking of the dawn.
I cry then,
for no reason that I can explain.
I drink whisky,
hold a cigar between my lips
where sometimes her lips are.

Sometimes, when the moon is in full veil
and flowing coat,
I want to lift my arms in worship
to the taste of love
that tumbles down from the sky.
I want to feast at its table
and take my fill;
yet I am dying of starvation
and I do not know why
– except that love is impossible
to consume or to hold,
it comes when it will
and that's when her eyes swallow me;
her brown eyes,
and we are hungry together.

It is so quiet here
beneath the sky and the darkness
and I wonder how something as big as the moon,
as big as love,
makes no noise.
I listen right through the long hours
and never tire of the silent conversation
even though I can't make sense of the words;
they come like whispered kisses,
captured commando style by the stillness,
and they give shape to the promise
that lies beneath the teasing fabric of her skirt.

The fragile sheen of the silver-blue light
is broken by the wheels of the long haulers
ripping across the bitumen.
The moon knows their story,
knows the love that is layered
at every turn of the highway,
knows the layovers,
the stopovers,
the wrong turns
and the dead-end streets,
like I know the touch of her hand,
like she knows the rise in the road;
like she knows
both the cruelty and the grace.

Through the heaviness of sleep
and the breathless path
of shooting stars and restless dreams,
there remains that one love
that outlasts all others;
it lives under the watchful eye of the moon
and does not break under the blow of pickaxe
or hammer
or distance
or time
or space
or feather.
And she is my moon,
my fledging harvest of love,
my dirt road
and my heart kept.

Rose Northey (she/her) is a Tāmaki Makaurau-born poet, illustrator and comedian living in Te Whanganui-a-Tara. She has performed at TEDx Auckland, was runner-up at the 2020 NZ National Poetry Slam and won the 2020 Going West Poetry Slam. Rose's hybridised art and poetry is featured in *Catalyst* and can be found in her growing collection of written and illustrated zines. Rose's illustrations for her first children's book, *The Lighthouse Princess* by Susan Wardell (Puffin, 2022), won the Storylines Gavin Bishop Award and it made the Whitcoulls Kids Top 50 list.

Salt and Vinegar and Shame

It's pathetic that I writhe in the eyes of other
drivers in the short stint from the supermarket.   Yes
I have three packets of chips sitting shotgun but
they are not just   for me. Three is a very respectable
potluck portion, all of them untouchable before 6.30, which
is a very respectable time for eating chips   okay?

I've got to watch it with the Salt and Vinegar though. There's
this growing electricity between us. It's a kind of chemistry,
so many   sodium,   hydrogen ions   teasing me.

You present as a wholesome wholegrain. Proper with
a '*BAKED NOT FRIED!!*' tagline at your neck, worn like
a top button collar,   but I don't buy it. A compound copulating
poppy seeds and MSG could only be called illicit. You are so
bad for me, you probably have like 1000 calories.

I pull into a side street to pick up a friend. I send a text
into the crackling air, *'Here where U at?'*,   and it trails
an ellipsis unanswered and it hails an oasis to
hypotheticalities. So fertile is a silence in the spawning of
forming desires and they settle as spittle to tongue and

snippets from a past life assail me. It's classic, the guilty
cracks in my composure tend to let the Catholic out, *'Please
do not feed the fantasies. You need to keep the door
open, noggin occupied, stick to populated places as well.'*

OH my dogmatic conscience can you really not tell that I hold
my graces ornamental now, the rosary only a necklace now,
my heathen mind finds a different definition for the fingering
of beads. There is nothing left to stall the parting pucker of

your lips   the give of you to smoothness on my tongue   just one
and one and one and one to find the sating weight of you inside
me   pinning the wings of butterflies in my stomach   someone is
coming   someone is coming   quick

You slip into the back seat unfinished, a chuckle in the crinkle
of your packet. I catch a flash of parted foil open to the air
left to spill the scent of shame   and vinegar   and salt.

Hatched and grown in California, **Redwood Reider** (they/them) came to Aotearoa in 2005 for a research fellowship, sprouted new roots and has lived here ever since. Redwood often collaborates with live musicians and has performed across Aotearoa at music festivals and a huge diversity of other events. They have released four full-length albums of poetry with music: studio recordings *Sacred Activist* (2015) and *Poetree* (2011), and live albums *Live from the Forest Floor* (2021) and *A Process of Love & Rhyme* (2009).

Got tired of explaining my pronouns so I wrote this poem

standing in a metal elevator,
i step forward to press the button, close the doors.
'attaboy' the old man says.
i chuckle inwardly.
upon more detailed anatomical inspection, he issues a correction:
'sorry, attagirl.'
cringe. nah mate
wrong again.

facebook used to have 20 different checkboxes for gender
but i just wanted to write 'tree'
deconstructing grammar
before grammar
deconstructs
me.

i just find it queer
to refer to every human constantly as he or she
as though a parcel of genitals
is what walks down the street.
i'm a human tree
i got roots for feet

why
should the molecules of this i
need an either/or when my
trunk is grown in earth and my
lips are smeared with sky?

i remember the first time
someone called me 'they'
as i stepped onto a stage.
i felt my shoulders grow wings,
toes wiggle
a little deeper

into this earth,
like i'd just stepped out of
someone else's scratchy clothes.
so let's unbutton those
concepts they're chafing my psyche
old fabrics
from the coloniser patriarchy.

how many indigenous tapestries
have known the holy
in they, we beasts who
blur the lines?

this bodymind
is a hologram
sirma'am
and gender is not a spectrum it's a kaleidoscope
trans/cending anatomy
trans/formative
trans/boundary.

if this seems a big adjustment
for a monkey mind to make,
consider that our eyes
see everything upside down
then flip it right.
so i reckon we can
adjust our
bi-noculars
to deliver some inner sight.

oh and by the way
i'm still extremely gay
cos I got a thing for my fellow trees –

see language is a game!
we make it up
as we go along
if the rules don't work
the rules can break
no one's in charge
it's just a game

and every moment our brains rewire into the shape
of what we articulate

our neurons tongues lungs weave this
collective space

so how about breathing a place
in which all our kin
can breathe fully
in their our own skin?

what do you reckon?
and speaking of you
why do you keep using the pronoun 'i' to refer to your self?
only 10 percent of the cells that you call 'me' enclose your own DNA
we're all seething ecosystems made of microorganisms
so hey
doesn't that make you
more of a they?

the community of cells known as 'me'
moves through forest.
in the eyes of my fellow trees,
i we perhaps perceived
as an ambling sack of fluids
emanating love songs, sweaty smell,
stream of urine sinking into soil,
a mouth exhaling
carbon dioxide
that plants breathe in.
what a relief
just to be
a walking ecology
among fellow trees

and okay.
if you don't want to call me they.
one could instead accurately say
i am a dance of electrons
a cloud of living memories
a cybernetic web of impulses thoughts feelings
a living expression of earth's dream
of healing
four limbs, lungs, rivers of blood
thumping heart
sparkly eyes
furry bark
a candle of poetry
glowing in the dark

language can't do much.
these fingers scribbled these lines by
pastel palette of sunset lapping a sandy beach
melting yellowpink ripples
fluctuating
beyond what my vocabulary of colour can speak
but at least it's an honest living
knowing this liquid nowness
fizzing round my salty ankles is
forever
mystery.

give me A or B
i choose both
and neither/nor
A or B?
i choose C
the vast sea
that sees
from within the casing of this skin,
a being with two legs
standing on earth
exhaling galaxies of love through words.
kia ora my name is redwood,
assigned human at birth.

Ray Shipley is an Ōtautahi-based comedian, poet and professional book-pusher. In 2019, Ray was nominated for the Billy T. James Comedy Award, a gong that recognises emerging comedians with outstanding talent. Ray has won the Christchurch Poetry Slam four times, and was placed third nationally in 2018. Their poetry can be found in the anthologies *Solid Air: Australian and New Zealand Spoken Word* (University of Queensland Press, 2019) and *Out Here: An Anthology of Takatāpui and LGBTQIA+ Writers from Aotearoa* (Auckland University Press, 2021). Since 2020, Ray has been running Late Night Poetry Hour regularly at Little Andromeda – a celebration of poetry and feelings and staying up past bedtime.

This poem was first published in *Catalyst* 19 (2022).

I AM WATCHING THE STRAIGHT COUPLES HOLIDAYING BY THE POOL

I am watching the straight couples
holidaying by the pool,
their skin browned & shining &
sticking slightly to the water-resistant material
of the lounger.

I am watching him order her another cocktail &
I hear him make some vulgar comment about
pineapple.
She throws her head way sun-umbrella back &
laughs & laughs & laughs.
Touches him.
Later, in the shallow & warm water, she suckles on his largest toe.
Makes eye contact with the waiter carrying her fifth piña colada.

I am watching the straight couples holidaying by the pool,
& I resent them because
every day before I go to the pool I find ways of
making my body less & less
present.
My love & I do not hold hands
I have shaved & hacked away at my hair so I am dolphin-like
I hold my book in a way that disguises my stomach.
Our shared intimacy is a raised eyebrow.

I am watching the straight couples holidaying by the pool.
He presses his body onto her as he kneads lotion into her shoulders.
They moan, quietly.
I look away.

Let it be known: I do not resent affection.

I resent powerful men behaving as if
affection is something they own; direct; control.
I resent the stare he gives us when we return to our shared room.

Tomorrow, I will begin to grow my leg hairs.
Tomorrow, I will put on a button-down shirt again.
Tomorrow, we will hold hands.

Tomorrow.

Jordan Hamel is a writer and performer from Aotearoa. He was the 2018 NZ National Poetry Slam champion and represented Aotearoa at the World Poetry Slam champs in California. In 2022, he published his debut poetry collection *Everyone is Everyone Except You* (Dead Bird Books) and co-edited *No Other Place to Stand: An Anthology of Climate Change Poetry from Aotearoa New Zealand* (Auckland University Press). He is currently completing an MFA at the University of Michigan Helen Zell Writers' Program on a Fulbright Scholarship. He owes his success to the New Zealand performance-poetry scene and the friends and enemies he's made along the way.

This poem was first published in *Everyone is Everyone Except You*.

God doesn't watch you anymore

Have you ever had your flatmate walk in while you masturbate? It's that, except your flatmate is an eternal omnipotent being who's probably not real. A voyeur disgusted by your every pubescent impulse, who instead of shutting the door and leaving you to your shame just kind of stands there and maintains eye contact.

That won't stop you. Because it's 2006, the perfect storm – unrelenting hormones and dial-up internet. The only computer sits in the lounge, with a stage-5 LimeWire virus and a screensaver collage of your dead grandmother.

You plan a heist of your father's magazines, so meticulous it would make Danny Ocean proud, you didn't even require a plot device masquerading as Julia Roberts. You have 20 minutes before Dad's home. Let's face it: you've come too far not to.

But now it's 2022

God doesn't watch you anymore

God closed his eyes the moment you delivered a sermon
inside someone else's skin.

God can't hear you anymore

You are Moses, preaching the 10 Commandments
in leather and sweat.

God won't speak to you anymore

They write psalms on the back of your head
face down in childhood pillows.

God doesn't want you anymore

Your mouth performs pagan rituals on borrowed mattresses.
The discoloured sheets, your Shroud of Turin.

God doesn't need you anymore

You have all the guilt you'll ever need.

God can't find you anymore

If Jesus were around now would he eat ass like the rest of us?
If he was, you'd let him watch.

You'd show him the repressed normativity
he always wanted for you. He'd watch you
slip off your wrinkled shirt, your playful socks,
slide lazily into bed, distracted by the housing crisis,

put on some Coldplay

Lights will guiiiiide you home

light a hummus-scented candle

and igniiiiiite your bones

stare deeply into her eyes, safe in the systemic income disparity

and I will try

think of the All Blacks/cum uncontrollably

to fix you

Eric Soakai is a performance poet based out of South Auckland, who is of Tongan (Pangai, Ha'apai) and Samoan (Poutasi, Falealili) descent. They were awarded the Banff Indigenous Art Residency in 2020 and have won slams including the 2019 NZ National Poetry Slam. Eric has work published in various places, most notably with *Knowledge Makers Journal* 6 (2021).

An Ode to Nostalgia

I wish I could go back,
back to 1 20 pics from the dairy
back to road patrol and library duty.
When dollar sausage sizzles were ALL THE RAGE,
And BULLRUSH
                bullrush was, just as much as it did the tacklers,
                                                            as much as the teachers on the sides.

I wish I could go back,
to hop scotch and tamagotchis
Jump jam!
But never really jump jam, we danced our own moves
because ours
were ten times better.

Back to bed times and nursery rhymes.
When telling Susie she had cooties basically meant you liked her.
Maybe . . . this is my confession I think she had cooties
Maybe . . . I actually liked her.

I wish I could go back,
to when Scribe couldn't stay off the charts!
And trampolines didn't have safety nets
and the biggest philosophical debate,
was 'whether your dad could bash my dad?'
But we all know
NONE of your dads could bash my dad.
Because my dad had the meanest moustache of the 70s
I swear it gave him superpowers.

I wish I could go back,
to BRICK PHONES
and that awkward tap tap tapping when you were texting your crush and there was never enough internal memory to store anything, so you had to delete everything!

                                                Except for that one text

that made you feel like you were the Skux-Deluxe,
'Skux-Master-General' type of person.

I want to go back,
to when early mornings were for cartoons
and late nights were for sleepovers,
and passing out on the sofa
didn't mean you were drunk.
You were simply tired.

I will forever treasure those fleeting moments.
The impermanence found in nostalgia,
flicking through the photo film of yesteryear
watching the memories dry up and freeze.

Situated within time and event
I will forever cherish the joy
as
it
seeps
through
my
fingertips.

Living in a world that   will   not   stop   dancing
Even when I'm sweating in places sweat does NOT deserve to be.

This is my ode to nostalgia,
to the childhoods we remember through rose-tinted glasses,
and the actuality of those childhoods we survived.

To the BFFLs we have, had and lost
who live on in our dearest recollections.

To the bruised knees from falling out of trees
'Mum and Dad, can I stay the night
PLEASEEEEEEEEEEEEEEEEEEEEEEEEEEEEEEEEEEEEEEEEEEEEEEEEEEEEEE?'
Spaghetti and cheese toasties
that classified us as Master Chefs.

This is to the one hour, two hour
Boyfriend, Girlfriend, Special-friend,
Partners we all had. That some of 'us' still have . . .

This is to the pillow forts that stretched an endless horizon
and the beds they sprouted out of.

I hope you find yourself back there!!!
In that space,
dreaming and thinking in colours we aren't sure even exist.
But backing yourself, the way your childself deserves to be backed.

Kasi Valu (Ma'ufanga, Lapaha, Tonga) is a Toi Whakaari graduate whose first love of storytelling is acting. As an actor, poet, writer and an assistant producer for Le Moana under the leadership and vision of Tupe Lualua, Kasi's work currently centres on the experiences, wit, complexities and universality of the Pasifika galaxies. Kasi appeared in *Withstand* (2017) and *Tales of a Princess* (2019) both by Suli Moa, and in *Brown Crown* (2021) by Sarai Perenise-Ropeti, wrote *L.U.T.E Lies Underneath The Earth* (2021) and produced *Shifting Centre* (2022–2023) directed by Oto Lupo and Safa Tunupopo. In 2020, Kasi co-founded Talanoa Toko, a creative collective built on kinship, sharing conversation in their falekā through recorded episodes. In 2021, Kasi placed first and was awarded the people's choice award at the E Tū Whānau Spoken Word Competition and received a Tautai Fale-ship residency. Kasi's work has been published in *Viva, The Big Idea* and *Vernacular*.

Ipu Tī

Uncanny faces circle the mattresses and chairs I call home
Outside are 8 pairs of slippers, inside there are 3 couches
The jandals painted white on the brown balm of each sole, ribboned with red and blue leather straps

I've seen these ones at Ōtāhuhu, they sell them next to the talo
I've seen my Nena wear this to the flea market
I've seen my Nena swing this like a helepelu slicing wild spring onions when my brother gets lippy

Yesterday was Saturday,
I know because I can smell baked talo leaves and the juice of plums wedged between slats of dough
Excommunicated hands get slapped for reaching, the answer is no
I woke up to the hum of prayers shifting the couches around
Nena tells me to boil the kettle, and plate the Super Wine biscuits,
she winks at me to save the Krispie coconut cookies for later

Everyone in the lotofale pouts their lips and scratches the air like a wild cat,
encouraging me to kiss them
I see no point in doing so but they insist
I only do so for the Krispie coconut cookies waiting for me in shelf above the microwave
Only Nena can reach them so I have to be good
2 tablespoons, not teaspoons of sugar
Chelsea commands mills that toss and turn the sap of sugar canes blowing in the humid breeze across salty waters
My Nena told me our people were traded like sheep to farm the seeds for Chelsea, just for us to have sugar in our cups
That's why it's 2 tablespoons

The scent of the room is confusing
A concoction of musky cologne
Coconut oil
Warm ashy feet
Victoria's Secret body lotion and mist
Nena beams her eyes,
Cutting through the glass cabinet
Adorned with family photos that partition the kitchen and the lounge
I return the Bell Tea box into the cupboard
Wistfully scamper to the kettle and open the glass jar compressed with Twinings Earl Grey

Everyone prefers their tea without milk
Pure black tea
The universe wanted to conspire trials to test the emptiness of my stomach
Volcanic branding on my wrist masked by a searing smile if I trip over the fala
I remember last time it burned my hand,
I popped my bubble too early
and it got infected
I had to stay in my room,
I couldn't leave the house

Tulou is your safe word, passing through valleys of whispering aunties with bulging eyes
Passing through shiny bald heads lathered in Nivea cream and Joop
The men sit on the floor, their legs crossed like crispy caramel pretzels
A man holding an apple-green rosary stretches his leg out like a tired vine screeching for the warmth of the sun
Pivot, swivel, head down, smile and the safe word
The patele is served first, he sits on my Grandpa's chair,
Nobody is allowed on that chair, It's like trying to replant a hibiscus in winter, Nobody is allowed to sit in my Grandpa's chair
My smile fades
Ika'i !
Have I done something wrong?
The safe word, it must be my smile
Twinings?

The patele smiles and speaks with his eyes
I nod my head and serve the woman perched on the couches
Dressed in assortments of black lace, embellished with flowers
foreign to the soils of my Nena's garden
Emulating the curtains that decorate each window sill

Marked with crimson red lipstick that sticks to the hairs on my cheek like candle wax I am loved beyond measure
I glide with grace back to the microwave with my prize towering above my head

I wait
They begin singing my favourite song
I feel mafana
My feet begin to melt and my eyes swell with tears
The cupboard creaks open, it required cautionary care with the rusty iron screws
that barely hold the box together
I feel lips barbed with cactus thorns pressed against the top of my head
My grandpa towers over the rivers that stream down my face
He hands me the Krispie coconut cookies
Nena's last packet saved for me, a taste that transports her home in one bite

Moefiainu Feagai Fenunuivao Daisy Lavea-Timo a.k.a. Daisy Speaks stands on the shoulders of a long line of orators, preachers and teachers from Vailu'utai, Samatau, Saipipi and Germany. She is dedicated to holding Vā space and amplifying the voices of rangatahi and storytellers of Te Moana-nui-a-Kiwa. Daisy is a Read NZ Writers in Schools facilitator, trustee of WORD Christchurch, curator of *Confluence* – an indigenous showcase of music and poetry – and 2017 NZ National Poetry Slam champion. Daisy serves as a tulafale (speaking chief) and has performed at TEDx Christchurch, Auckland Speaks, Queensland Poetry Festival, Cairns Art Festival, education conferences and with her flautist/poet daughter Micahlei Timo.

LAEI

An 'au – chisel has bitten my skin
And his black marks tell this tale
of Siamese demi-gods singing
E tatā o Fafine ae le tatā o Tane *(Only the women get tattooed)*
Diving for enchanted treasures they messed the lyrics up and sang
E tatā o Tane ae le tatā o Fafine *(Only the men get tattooed)*

The breeze nonchalantly does the *'Wassup uce!'* around the Apia faleo'o
My game face is Seki and I'm expiring,
I mean perspiring! Just-a-little!

This is it. There is no turning back.

The Tufuga walks in with the swagger of a lead actor
takes out his Hollywood kit and lays out his 'Au Ta
'Are you reddi?'
Handing him the gifts, I nod.
Su'a Sulu'ape Paulo Junior is Taika Waititi,
3-in-1 actor, producer and director
Motifs etched in his brilliant mind; all he draws on my thighs are 3 lines

Middle
Left **Right**

'Breef in and houllld!'
As I breeeeeathe in, his support actors stretch my skin
Sulu'ape picks up his hammer and his chisel and he
Tap-tap-taps black lines all the way down, he
Tap-tap-taps black lines all the way down
His support actors wipe my blood with a damp, muslin cloth

I breathe in Sky and he **tap-tap-taps**
Fetū stars and Gōgō frigate birds
I breathe in Sea and he **tap-tap-taps**
Ave'au starfish and Alualu jellyfish
I breathe in Land and he **tap-tap-taps**
Anufe caterpillars and Toluse crosses
The Vae'ali headrests and Atualoa centipedes crawl down the backs of my knees
Service of the past + service of the future + service of the untitled
>< Aiga >< Church >< Village >< Nation >< World ><

E toa lou loto? They said
See I have not yet met the woman I am becoming
I know that She stands on the shoulders of Giants
She is the ribcages of Salamasina Queens and Nafanua Warriors
She is Cookie, building Empires with the hustle of a Beast mode bloodline
She is the Falelua o le Aiga Malofie
Who when Tatau was threatened with colonialism
        She
blasted her gangster music, sculled some Ava and stood with her Tane
She fought for these Ancestral Marks of Mana
for these defiant Scripts, Texts and Testimonies
of Nationalism and Beauty.

E toa lou loto? They said
And as he **Tap-tap-taps . . . . TAP-TAP-TAPS . . . . TAP-TAP-TAPS**
my kneecaps
I understand why . . . If I can handle this . . .
Giiiiiiiiiiirrrrrlllllllll!!!
I can handle Anything!
There is no turning back
I have made that sacred Covenant, between
Being Sāmoan & Living Sāmoan
I am Malu – Diamond
I am Malu – Shade
I am Malu – Shield
I am Malu – Shelter
I am Malu – Protector
I am Malu – Nurturer
I am Malu
I Am Malu
I AM MALU
O le Laei o le tama'ita'i Sāmoa
The adorning of a Sāmoan Queen

Ruby Lupe Ah-Wai Macomber navigates multiple indigenous and diasporic identities in her whakapapa to Rotuma, Taveuni, Ngāpuhi, Scotland and Germany. She was awarded a New Zealand Society of Authors Mentorship in 2018, was runner-up in the University of Auckland Poetry Slam in 2021, recipient of a New Zealand Young Writers Festival micro-residency in 2022 and University of Auckland Arts Student of the Year in 2022. Her work is published in *Landfall*, *Kete Books*, *Starling*, *Signals*, *Taumata Rau* and *Awa Wāhine*. Ruby facilitates Te Kāhui, a Corrections- and community-based creative writing programme for rangatahi. She advocates for Pink V, mandarins without seeds and is currently working on a collection exploring Rotuman diasporic experiences in Aotearoa.

Se Fua

in my grandmother's tongue
when we sneeze
we say
            se fua
please

do not burst open

poise at the floodgates that moment longer
and breathe   just one more time

and should we choose to honour the love
we both deserve
let this be a conversation

wait
    and our words, they will play together

watch them burst in the back seat
Kolohe Kai on repeat
KFC, we'll eat
and we'll laugh

sip Pepsi from plastic wine glasses
pull chicken flesh from the gaps in our smile

in my grandmother's tongue
we know love in motion
            Hanisiof
I love   across an ocean
            an island
I have never set eyes on

I am a daughter of the diaspora
        but my tūpuna insist
on coating my tongue in apei mats

Fakpeje on a Friday
woven gods speak to the earth in cupped-hand claps
we'll practise
being good descendants today

        Hanisiof
sometimes this love cannot cling to empty English
so we torture our tongues
tell them **they** are unworthy
trip, spit and stutter between languages
        because this love
        because this love

because I heard my father's Rotuman tongue lay flaccid when his mother died
his words
they had no one to play with anymore

Se fua
her funeral was the first time I saw him

        burst
Se fua
        Please
Se fua
        Please
Se fua
        Please
Se fua
        please

do not burst on me

in my grandmother's tongue
we know love in motion
        Hanisiof
map our lives according to all those
we have ever loved
back to our mother's fonua
the land
        the first thing that ever loved us
this love stretches from the atua
to Hawaiki

        across oceans

and open palms

to my nan and her tapa skin
massage the knotted histories from her neck
and trust they've held more than just her head up

half-peeled mandarins left in the fruit bowl
and the rosary on her pillow

we pray
Catholicism is our first language

isa lei
sing to her grave
Hanisiof

she is the love
I wish did not pass in motion

love stumbles in different tongues
but the blue persists in our veins

we
must not be far from the ocean now,

one day
our words
they will play together again
and cry together again
kneel at the altar for communion   together again

Hanisiof
when we sneeze,
say *se fua*
please
do not burst

but resurface
gasping and giggling
strong in yourself, your tenacious tongue

speak and love
in grandmother's tongue

Renee Liang 梁文蔚, a second-generation Cantonese New Zealander, is a paediatrician, poet, playwright and essayist who works on theatre, poetry, fiction, visual arts works, dance, film, opera, community events and music. She was an MC at Poetry Live for four years. Her major works include eight plays, three chapbooks of poetry and a memoir on motherhood. *The Bone Feeder* (2008) was commissioned by Auckland Arts Festival in 2017 as an opera with music by Gareth Farr. In 2018 she was appointed a Member of the New Zealand Order of Merit for services to the arts. She lives in Tāmaki Makaurau.

Chinglish

Yesterday
a shop lady smiled at me
and said,
'Your English is very good,'

her eyes crinkled
in a let's-be-nice-to-aliens way.

I wanted to say

– of course it bloody is,
– I was born here,
– how about you?

But of course I said nothing.
hardly her fault
we Asians all look the same
anyway.

Maybe I should have
I AM KIWI
tattooed on my forehead
except then
I'd be told off by my mother.

My mother.

When I was born
I slept in Chinese
I fed in Chinese
I cried in Chinese

pooed in Chinese even.

Mother and Father
left their English
lying around the house
like lollies

they knew I wouldn't touch
I was good then.

We kids built houses
with wooden blocks
painted with Chinese characters.
We fought over
longer characters
on bigger blocks,

better for building walls.

My mother used to say,
'No talking English at home!'

I'd brought it home like a disease
from kindy
and infected my sisters.

By the time we were teenagers
my mother was getting tired
from yelling
'No English!'

Once my sister and I decided to start speaking French.
We thought we were being smart.
Even though we weren't too good at French.

English was my camouflage.
As long as I wore it
talked in English
dreamt in English
ate in English
yes,

even shit in English
I couldn't be too Chinese

could I?

In Hong Kong
I am swept along the pavement
by a torrent of Cantonese
and shop ladies crinkle their eyes
in a let's-be-nice-to-aliens way.

'Your Chinese is good,'
they say,
'for a foreigner.'

Marina Alofosio is a Samoan poet based in South Auckland, originating from the villages of Mulifanua, Leauva'a, Faleasiú and Falefa. She has performed locally and internationally for varied events including Nuyorican Poets Café, TEDx Auckland, Adelaide Fringe, Toronto Writers Festival and the New Zealand Government Apology for the Dawn Raids Ceremony. She has received artist residencies with Banff Creative Arts Institute and Tautai Arts Trust. Marina wrote three shows with the Black Friars theatre troupe between 2018 and 2021, released her first music single, 'We Want the Dawn', in 2021 and has a short story published in the journal of literature and art *IKA* 4 (2016).

Eviction

You could stand on the peak of a statehouse and call it a mountain
Drop down the sails of your ravaged RAV4 and call it, *Malaga*
I'm in that place between homelessness and real living
Cos it's only when the spirit is broken that I go looking for refuge

You could sleep on the floor next to your children
All of us laying side by side on a king single mattress and call that provision
There's an intake for sleepless mothers at the Manukau courts
But I'm not watching children split into pavements down into root prejudice
My children's shelter is right here in my vigilance

The census can't tell you this
But we actually come from a fisherman's village, *Mulifanua*
From what I know, there is no gold mine under the seabed where my father's fishing rod leapt
He travelled 3000 km to the next shore to find land
I know I have the endurance to pick up where he left

Somewhere on this whenua is a home

Perhaps in the heart of South Auckland where my head rests the most
In these streets that reverb the cadences of almost-men or perhaps
In East Auckland where gentrification is a burning bush
Somewhere in the alleyway of Exodus is the promise

We are hardly starving, barely living, yet just beginning to wonder
How you can make something out of nothing
Cities out of words
Meals out of mystery
Fortunes out of failure

The census can't tell you this
But my babies and I belong to a Kingdom dream, *Mau*
And right above our heads as we sleep into surrender
Is a golden canopy stretching the tent pegs of our imagination

Rex Letoa Paget (Samoan–Danish) is a fa'atama skuxx crafter of words born in Aotearoa. His storytelling and poetry are his compass through space and time, as he journeys through loss, grief and shame that have been learned growing up in a capitalist, colonial society. His works are lessons, learnings and acknowledgements for past, present and future timelines. Rex's words are gifts from his ancestors that have been published in *Tupuranga*, *Stasis*, *Te Tangi A Te Ruru* and *No Other Place to Stand: An Anthology of Climate Change Poetry from Aotearoa New Zealand* (Auckland University Press, 2022).

Everything is Everything
after Ms Lauryn Hill

to know your sweetness is
to know where you lay and
feed the trees.

where you recognise
handprints embossed in
molten rock by first frosts.

where you become
witching-hour stories told
around plastic tables on
moss-covered patios and
stardust glistening on the nose
of your wildest dreams.

to know your sweetness is
to know the structure of your
bones.

cheeks cut from Atlantic
fjords and nurseries of
nana Nielsine's grit
fighting fires in pit-sawn
huts, hid her eleven children
and husband down a well
while pregnant with her twelfth.

eyes carved from first blast
uranium and your father's
love of the chase
crooked-eared coasts
of your greats
who sawed rings for their hands.

tinkerers of forests and sands
fine ground rushing thru
hourglasses. time kept close
fisted behind their backs.
sifting through secrets
stashed in cul-de-sacs
dead named facts.

what lies beneath
what they don't teach is
fungi forest fabric marbled
with fine pandanus linens
covering bellies of rebellion mothers
where you were dreamed of.

you,
secret-seer
moon-believer
shadow-greeter.

paved the road from your front door
with a 6 to 1 mix of curiosity and nerve.
biting fear til you can see your fingertips
finding clues Nana Heather left you
on postcards and backs of photographs.

notice your hands in
seamstresses
weavers
painters
teachers.

weaving past and future
through bows of your bind
til you can sit present
anchored
in the gravity of time.

crossed-legged with mum
as she teaches you
how to plait grass.
twisting life into a
high-waisted season
acid wash
flared denim
belt looped over

silk-webbed patchwork
stitched beneath skin
since before wind
whispered into mountain.

painting your dad's bedroom
galactic black.
fishing for stars of his youth.
singing on the back
of his 61 triumph
vinyl planets spinning
45 rounds per minute

god save the queen
the fascist regime
they made you a moron
a potential h-bomb

malcolm mclaren meets
johnny rotten
spitting seeds of his adam's apple
not far from trees in his back yard
you pull weeds off
freeing your breath
in unison.

you,
made of
mangrove forests
lightning-scarred winds
high tides polishing
rocks in the sky.

familiar pull of belly button
waking you in the middle of the night.
following fleets of hawks until
you can smell home.
burnt pine and damp forest
floor on an open fire.

charcoal eyes send
smoke signals to curses
brass knuckled between
your fingers. each one a dark
alley bruise on ripe flesh.
slugging it out in

hand-me-down sweaters.
picking apart the yarn of
truth when it lays you flat.

realising you aren't all of your
ancestors' wildest dreams.
for some, you're probably
their worst nightmare.

breaking fingers that curl
around empty forks on
hungry east coast roads.
rewiring the matrix in your brain.
drowning your given name.

your veins do not lie in vain.

lifetimes from now
when your grandmothers
begin to cloak themselves
in leaves their favourite colours
new hands will search
the vine to find you.

they will dig through
dust gathered at seams
of forgotten salvation pockets.

pickaxe pixels from
a capsule of memories
planted in fields named
after your children.

catch your lessons on
the bridge of their nose
you cross
to come home.

Jessica Arcus loves the way writing poetry can bring clarity, beauty and hope to the often-unspoken things in life. She is relishing finding her voice again as an adult and, after performing at her first open mic night in her hometown of Ōtautahi a year ago, is hooked on speaking her poems out loud. She came runner-up at the 2022 Ōtautahi poetry slam and her work has been published in *Catalyst*.

Enclosed

These two hands
have been enclosed by Pa's
oversized and calloused
farmer's fingers,
felt the fragility
of sun-drenched blackberries,
caressed keys in such a way
as to rouse tears from dim blue eyes,
tracking down well-creased cheeks –
soft, like warm rising dough.

How do these hands
forget such things have blessed them –
been blessed by them,
to commit such sacrilege
against themselves;
skin and sinew and bone clasping
flesh of my flesh,
graceless,
a weakness I can't look in the eye.

A loss of orientation must
masquerade as something
and here it looks like domination
– it is loud, it is ugly,
here it is damnation.

Come, come hands,
let me enfold you
oh I will hold you
close to my chest
to my lips
to my breath
and I will utter only softness,
kiss you over and over
and my tongue
it won't stop pouring out upon you
the scent of blooming cabbage trees
and warm harakeke flowers
and the feeling of your young body
wading through
thigh-high grasses,
summer-dry,
lone roaming under blushing skies.

Cleave to me,
sweet palms
and this will be your song
and we will be one
and you'll find yourself home.

Henrietta (Etta) Bollinger is a Pākehā writer, performer and disabled-community advocate. They first began performing their poetry in 2009 and their poems have been published in *Starling, Mimicry* and *Scum*. Their plays have been staged in Aotearoa, Australia and England. Henrietta has deep gratitude for the space that was created in the Rising Voices Youth Poetry Slam workshops, which allowed them to have confidence in their voice and they continue to have friendships from that time.

This poem was developed in the inaugural Rising Voices Youth Poetry Slam workshop and was first published in *Salient*, as part of Henrietta's column 'Token Cripple'.

Let the Metal Beast Sulk

You've been down –
Maybe it's just that you have to be close to the ground for the world to speak –
so the things you hear don't punch you any lower
because
there's bound to be
mud and blood and worm-halves
down there.

Ever since I started 'growing up'
there have been people teaching me
to rebel against *this* body
and sometimes I do.
But that's only when I forget to ask *why*.
Why they worry about the architecture of my soul
when they built the stairs that exist in my world.

Ever since I started 'growing up'
there have been people
teaching me to rebel against *this* body
and then you write to tell me
I have wings.

And some days,
we ditch the chair behind a tree,
let the metal beast sulk unseen.
You on guard, I lower myself to all fours

my arms –
cave
and though I sense you move
there is no flurry of panicked, motherly limbs
you *wait* to be asked.

I fall to commando in the grass,
arm, arm, drag legs
deliciously wet,
arm, arm, drag,
muddy shoes!
A perfect novelty,
arm, arm, drag legs, scuff shoes, scuff,
and I ask
Can we just stay here? Like forever?
Yeah. Why not?

Sara Hirsch (she/they) is a London-grown poet, a UK slam champion and ranked third in the World Slam Championships in 2014. She is a TEDx speaker, has performed at Glastonbury, the Edinburgh Festival Fringe and for the BBC. Sara has a Masters in Creative Writing and Education, has toured and taught poetry around the world and co-founded the national spoken-word organisation Motif Poetry Ruri Tūtohu. Sara has two published collections, *Still Falling* (Burning Eye Books, 2016) and *Louder Than Words* (BX3, 2017) and has work featured in *Magma, takahē* and *Poetry New Zealand Yearbook 2019*. She spends her time playing with her toddler while dismantling the patriarchy, one poem at a time.

This poem was first published in *The Anti-hate Anthology* (Spoken Word London, 2019)

A Poem about Being Human in Five Parts

I

Hey human, let me see your vulnerability. Fact. Putting shoes on in public is *such* an intimate act. Human sits in driver's seat, door flung in deliberate abandon, displays forbidden flesh of stranger's feet. Personalised number plate to match the surname, sneakers red to match the paintwork – perfect, toenails perfect, not a scratch, sneakers sneaky red to match the heat cheeky red to match the feet, red to spark the thought, to spark the smile, to spark the match.

Ankles naked to the wind, soles bared, squeezed in, laced up, this is activism on a Wednesday morning, this is skinny-dip driving. This is it. This is it. *Hey human, let me see your integrity, let me see your energy, let me see your grit. Let me see how easily your shoes don't fit.*

Did you know that you are being watched? Of course you do. Stupid question.

II

Shut up you stupid human.

You're a good driver, for a human.

Aren't you afraid that if you wear that people won't know you are a human?

Hey Human! Show us some leg!

Oh my god, you are such a strong, independent human, but you must get that all the time?
Your humanness is a bit distracting. Maybe tone it down a bit?

You should know your place, human.

Avoid the temptation to act like a human if you want to get ahead.

Maybe don't bother with humour – humans aren't very good at making people laugh, leave that to the humans, humans are just naturally funny.

Sorry, there is already a human on this panel. Sorry, we have already published one human this month. Sorry, we already have a human on our books. Sorry but the last human we had on just wasn't that popular, we aren't really prepared to take that risk again. Sorry, but this just wasn't really designed with humans in mind. You probably wouldn't like it anyway. Best leave this one to the humans, eh?

Oh, the human section is downstairs. You'll find it much more interesting. Don't worry yourself with all this.

Translation: This is no place for a human.

III

There is a voice you only use when you are explaining Facebook to your mother.

There is a face that you only pull when you know that I am the only person watching. There is a face that you pull when you think I have turned away.

There is a voice you use when you want me to like you.

There is a voice you use when you don't care what I think.

There is a look you give me when I don't understand.

There is a name you call me that you think I like.

There is a name you call me that you know I don't.

There is a look that you give me when I have said something stupid.

There is a face you pull when I have got it wrong.

There is a word for that. There is a word for that. There is a word for that.

IV

Make a museum of me. I look great behind glass. I look so great, don't you think? Must be the arse. I look so great that everyone will want to look at me. You won't even have to advertise. Just put a picture of me at the entrance and people will flock, you'll see.

Make a museum of me. Call it educational. Call it whatever. Call it historically accurate. Call it well used. Name it after me.

Make a museum of me. Me, vintage car, British make and model, built to drive not to display No previous owners, despite what they say.

Make a museum of me. Make entry free, but compulsory. Play back the visits on the CCTV, prove they didn't touch, they never touched, just looked, just looked at me.

Make a museum of me. Line up my baby teeth in a neat little row, wind me up – see how far I go, invite the public, build a stage, call me entertainment. Go on, I dare you, put on a show.

V

Fingertips on glass, the smudge of shame, the smear of irresistibility only visible in the light, under the right kind of scrutiny.

A collection of fingernails exhibited in the back

dust circling in the stale air above. Once bitten, twice shy.

Once bitten, forever scarred. Once bitten, bite back.
The echo of this place, the emptiness, the unseen
potential.

Here is where we house our weakness,

notice how it blends into the architecture,

how it lets the light in,

how it holds itself up.

David Eggleton is a poet and writer based in Ōtepoti Dunedin. He has performed his poetry widely, won numerous awards and was New Zealand Poet Laureate 2019–2022. David's latest collection of poems is *Respirator: Laureate Poems 2019–2022* (Otago University Press, 2023).

This poem was first published in 2021 on the New Zealand Poet Laureate blog, administered by the National Library Te Puna Mātauranga o Aotearoa.

Matariki

Matariki's eyes are fiery in the night.
Feather-shawled mountains gleam their beaks.
Great trunks, sawn through, tumble and tilt.
Bold carvings, auctioned in whispers,
echo as prophecies, sung by wind-swept trees.
The hāngī steams Captain Cookers, basted in juices.
Plagued by caterpillars, slithered by eels,
a patchwork quilt of farm unravels.
In lightning and hail, each snail quivers;
learned visitors take shelter with skinks,
under rocks from nesting angry falcons.
Ghosts hoard waka in marshes, beneath silt.
An arcade is roofed with engraved glass;
a pedestal is bound by polished brass;
faces are wound tighter than a watchspring.
Wigs become a sheep flock gathering.
There's daughter of the kauri, Amber Reeves,
sailing for London from the Antipodes.
Through cavern gloom, suspended by ooze,
many worms glow as the matrix broods.

Jennifer Rockwell (she/they) is a poet and writer based in Tāmaki Makaurau. Her work has been published in *Poetry New Zealand Yearbook 2021* and *Symposia*. She won the 2017 WORD – The Front Line Slam, 2018 Going West Poetry Slam, 2021 JAFA Qualifying Slam, was runner-up in the 2021 JAFA Auckland Regional Finals and represented Tāmaki Makaurau at the 2021 NZ National Poetry Slam. Her writing often explores the intersection of queerness, the female experience and mental health.

Questions to Their Version of My God / In Response to Conversion Therapy

Dear God, I heard you were male.
So I was wondering
if people are made in your image, can I really trust you?
Cos I know of many men who say they eat your body daily,
but they still be doing ungodly things,
if they swallow your blood does that make them carnivores? Or blasphemous?

I've got a couple questions about your book?
One. How come the most holy women in it
are recognised for miracles involving their bodies?
Does this reflect the thoughts of the men who wrote it,
or of you?
Footnote: Is there a difference?
Two. Why are your boys so much like Thomas?
Always reaching to touch what they don't understand,
always sticking their hands in places they don't belong?
Three. Is it a sin for me to be comfortable
in my own skin?
Is it godly to be ashamed of the body you gave me?

Four. If Jesus came back now,
would we even recognise him?
Do you even recognise the paintings of you
we've got at church?
Does it offend you when we change the colour
of your Son's skin?
What if she came back as a woman,
would they let her preach?
Five. How come Eve emerged from the rib of Adam
when man only ever emerges from Woman?
Do I carry the shame of Eve?
Is there a way for me to separate my shame from hers?

Why did you give me this body?
In loving myself am I loving you?
Is it a sin for me to forgive myself?
Do I need to wait for you to do it?
What about that priest?
Did he ask for your forgiveness before or after he did
what had before been done to him?
Did you give him it? Do you love him?
How come I have to talk to him through a wall?
Is it to hide my shame, or his?

Do your scars look like mine? Do you feel rage? What do I do with all this rage?
How do I swallow my rage before it swallows me? Is anger good? Did you create anger? Are you angry?

Quickfire question:
Who do you identify with more?
The queer kid being sacrificed in your name,
or the father banishing his own kin,
baptising them in a suicidal shame?
Did Judith and those parents learn it from you?
That in being a parent, they inherit
the right to push their own child to want to die?

Is your heart breaking, too?
Are you hurting, like we are hurting?

Do you still shed a tear for every queer body, broken in your name?
Or are you used to it by now?
Did it become easier to watch us murder your children
after the first one?

Jahra Wasasala is a world-builder, movement psychopomp and writer of realms of Viti/Fiji and Palagi descent, based in Aotearoa New Zealand. Jahra utilises their training and specialisation within performance activation, various street-dance style techniques and poetic/voice soundscape as a psychopomp for their shapeshifting and storytelling through their public and personal embodiments. Jahra's solo and company works have toured throughout Aotearoa, Australia, Hawai'i, New York, Berlin, Guahån and Canada. Jahra has created commissioned embodiments for institutions including the Auckland War Memorial Museum, the Banff Centre in Calgary, the Smithsonian Museum in Washington DC and the Metropolitan Museum of Art in New York.

THE WORLD EATER & THE WORLD-SHAPER

truthfully, there is no greater horror than being born.

at this moment, I speak to You with half a body.
I am still collecting the rest, but there is enough of Me here to be visible
just as these words on this page are visible to You.

this half-body won't be able to satiate me for much longer.

so, before *You* and *I* become *We*
I will tell You the rules;

SAIVA:
this body is not (y)ours and They are/I am asking for it back.

DUA:
I am not a living thing. nor am I a dead thing. You are not a living thing, nor a dead thing.
remember this.

RUA:
there is more than one world. there is more than one memory. each maintains their own laws, their own first fall from the sun, their own approaching descent into madness. each sees through their own eyes.

TOLU:
I am sewn together through purified will
an aggregation of ruins,
possessed.
I moulded myself. I drew the borders around the beginnings and endings of my body
but I do not abide by any of them.

VA:
I am named before every loss.
I am named after every inheritance.
I am named in the vein
of what I am entitled to:
Dra.

>-+-<

as We are about to begin, it is already over
the sky has been burnt and blackened, filling Our mouth with ash and song

We hear it first
the sound of a tear in the fabric of this universe. the sound of laws being broken.

the tear that is made creates a living, pulsating wound
in time.
the wound opens like the universe's eye, scanning, surveying
unblinking, it begins to emit a disembodied scream scream scream scream scream scream
scream scream scream scream scream scream scream scream scream scream scream
scream
polluting the sky.

The Scream itself, like a liquid
pouring out of the wound, wrestling with its own form
a cluster of natural disasters adorned in a caliginous embryonic fluid
a ball of heat and light begins to form itself in the centre of The Scream
transforming into a force of *Yalo*, electricity, and semi-translucent matter
resisting the form
resisting the borders
The Scream's embryonic womb bursts with the pressure

The Scream is growing a head

then another
and another

sitting atop long writhing necks, the faces emerging on the armoured heads are never fixed.
if you think you can identify one, it mutates into something unrecognisable.
there is a face, and yet there is none. there is a body, and yet there is none.

The Scream rapidly crawls across the horizon like a lizard, tainting
everything it touches. The Scream is deliberate, dutiful, relentless
looking for Us.
The Scream knows Our scent, no matter what mask We choose within
whatever fleshy apparatus We are possessing.

The Scream stops their rampage across the sky. one of their heads catches Our eyes.

then another.

and another.

the air between Us and Them turns acidic.
a brief moment of acknowledgement

the multi-headed voice makes their way towards Us,
a body, gaining lifetimes in speed,
a body, carving a horizon bloody
jaws unhinging at the joints like old gates,
dragging the sky into the ground as they open.

We resist.

the closer The Scream gets,
the more We are pulled in
the more We are a collapsing star
being dragged into a black hole.

We resist

giving The Scream the charge it needs to begin The Breaking.

We resist

Our made-human-body surrenders
flesh howling
as it tears itself away from the bone,
the marrow within starting to boil
and leak, forming sacs of fluid erosion that corrupt
an already corrupted body

this should hurt.
this kind of pain should be enough to tear any embodied psyche apart.
this should be the kind of pain We have dreamt about.
but that does not matter
We cannot register any pain, because We are facing the only thing that We are afraid of;
[redacted]

attempting to escape doesn't help.

inhale.

the only thing that can be done is bracing on impact.

>–+–<

The Scream gently begins reversing their movements,
crawling backwards on its belly across the sky.
their heads retracting back into The Scream's first form of storms,
the embryonic fluid sealing it whole
until they are called upon again.
The Scream quietly slips back into the living rupture it was birthed from

the universe's eye,
an open witness to The Breaking,
closes,
the wound sealing itself as if nothing had been seen.

>–+–<

I spit out the ash and blood pooling in my throat until I am empty.

it is done.
I have been broken.
disembodied.
abandoned.

. . .
good.

I pull *the clown*'s mask out of Our remains
stitching it lovingly to where a human head of mine might be
laughing
as I begin to fill in the features with My chaos.

exhale.

We, are starved.
We, are loved.

let's begin.

again.

>–+–<

Danielle O'Halloran-Thyne is an Ōtautahi-born Samoan Pākehā (Irish/English) performance poet and co-founder of FIKA Writers collective. Danielle appears regularly in Ray Shipley's Late Night Poetry Hour at Little Andromeda, and her work can be found on SoundCloud and on the Christchurch Art Gallery Te Puna o Waiwhetū website as a complement to the exhibition Te Wheke: Pathways Across Oceania (2020–2022).

Replicon gods

The museums need us more than we need them, we have our ancestors inside us.
A palagi gets a prize for being an archaeologist / gynaecologist,
'. . . it's good these treasures / babies were saved even if they were stolen,' they said.
Museum gods save us like a severed head,
eating our mauli to feed their own
refusing an appropriate burial
so they can keep consuming, fat, with stolen mana.
They will eventually die in a flood, or a fire, or an earthquake, or a war,
or some new type of cancer.
The museum gods will turn to dust someday like us – me and the palagi,
we will be dust gods, ele'ele replicons,
giving birth giving birth giving birth.

Nadine Anne Hura (Ngāti Hine, Ngāpuhi, Pākehā) is a poet, essayist, zine maker and activist-by-stealth. Nadine's writing seeks to harness the power of indigenous storytelling to inspire collective action. Her work has been anthologised and performed widely, and she is a regular contributor to *The Spinoff*, *E-Tangata* and *Newsroom*. Nadine has received several literary awards including the Pikihuia Award in 2021 and the Michael King Writers Centre Emerging Māori Writers Residency in 2018. She is a part of the Wellington-based independent publishing collective, Taraheke, and is committed to opening space for other indigenous writers, artists and performers.

Truth

I keep going to kapa haka even though I can't sing.
I'm hopeless.
But I want to sing.
I want to.

I want to be the one who can swing the poi without dropping the poi but I'm always the one who drops the poi.

Lately I've begun to imagine my tūpuna are watching me, leaning against the wall and laughing, saying pai kare, that's our moko alright, two left wrists.

Sometimes I think I'm lost. I toss this way and that way in the storm but then words wash up on the shore and I pick them up, smooth like sea-glass in my hand.
Aro-hā.
Wai-rua
Whetūrangitia.

My nan's first language was Māori. Nanapā's first language was Māori. When people say we need to get over it I want to grab them by the shoulders and show them that this loss of ours was not gradual, it was sudden and violent and devastating. Imagine having the words stolen from your throat? That's what happened to our grandparents' generation and it changed how they thought and felt about themselves.

They were made to believe lies about who they were.

But I get the feeling people are sick of hearing about it. It's easier to sign up for a te reo course than it is to put the words back in someone else's throat.

The waiting lists at the wā are so long my mate missed out two years in a row. She and her tūpuna waited in a queue that snaked all the way out the door and down the steps only to take the train back home again empty handed.

I know I shouldn't be angry. Whose fault is it that our language suddenly got more popular than TikTok? After decades of being stamped out, shouldn't that make us happy?

I try not to be annoyed when my Pākehā classmates become fluent in the proper amount of time, or when they rush to answer questions that weren't directed at them, or correct someone else's mistakes.

They don't know that the most important thing is not showing everyone else how much they know.

I feel like my anger is mean-spirited and unjustified so I go back to the car after class and sit quietly in the dark with my tūpuna.

Mason Durie said that losing our language doesn't mean we lose our whakapapa. We don't lose our ways of connecting. We just find another way – another language, another vehicle.

None of us is ever truly lost. None of us.

Lately I've begun to feel my tūpuna reading over my shoulder when I write. They read closely, scanning each line for truth.

I can feel them breathing.

Sheldon Rua (he/they) is an emerging Māori Samoan fusion-performance poet and multidisciplinary creative born in South Auckland. He has performed at TEDx Manukau and the JAFA Poetry Slam, and his work has featured in Māorilands Film Festival, Someday Stories and Pou Kanohi at Auckland War Memorial Museum. He is a WORD – The Front Line alumnus and coach. Sheldon's mahi speaks largely to identity and culture and, through words, aims to perpetuate the shine that inherently lives within his communities.

Afa-tahi

I have heard
But not yet seen
So I press my ear to the empty moana in me
She, lay still
Waiting
Wading on the front doorstep of my arero
Like a māmā does for her tamariki
Like a karanga for her manuhiri
Haere mai, she calls
Haere mai
But he does not come
We have swallowed deep karakia for Io
But he does not come
We have made a bed, cuppa tea
But he does not come home

An orphan of the ocean
I watch the tide roll out
But it never comes back

How do you greet the faceless, when they do not want to be seen?
How do you greet the nameless, when they answer to no one?
How do you eat of the coconut, when you have not been taught to climb?

Te tohu o te rangatira, he manaaki, he tauawhi, he aroha
He kai nā te ringaringa whero i taka
Ko te kai a te rangatira, he kōrero,
E tama, hoki mai ki taku kāinga
You have spent decades hiding your face
Running from me
Only to realise Tangaroa and Tagaloa swim through us both

Come home

Tainui has carved safe passage

Come home

Come home

Hoki mai ki tō kāinga

Come home

Hoki mai ki au
I want to know you

Come home

Come home

Samoa
Toe fo'i mai ia te a'u

I've been waiting

ii.

Michael Moore is a descendant of Ngāti Maniapoto iwi, Tainui waka, Taupiri maunga and Waikato awa. He is a storyteller in service of his ancestors and weaves stories through creative collaboration. Michael was the director of the NZ National Poetry Slam from 2015–2017, co-founded the Uplift Poetry Tour (2014), founded and coordinated the Hamilton Poetry Slam for two years and co-created the multi-art form collaboration Ihirangaranga (2019). He placed second at the NZ National Poetry Slam in 2013 and the Going West Poetry Slam in 2017 and was a featured artist at The Red Dirt Poetry Festival (Alice Springs) in 2018. Michael was awarded the Banff Indigenous Art Residency in 2019.

RANGINUI

Sky Father, Koha
In a single breath
I take the sky into my lungs and carry clouds into my veins until a blueprint of my bloodline
maps a course on my skin, a route of trenches that run beneath the colony in my collagen
In a single breath
I drift from this urban myth back to my origin, for here they will try to tell me that my
whakapapa is a broken home, is criminality, theft, poverty, and violence
not love, royalty and pure divine guidance
My whakapapa is love, royalty, and pure divine guidance
Our whakapapa is love, royalty, and pure divine guidance
Koha
to press our nose against the sky is to elude mortal bonds
to press our nose against each other is to infuse mortal bonds
a gift in a single breath.

Ngā Hinepūkōrero is a group of four wāhine Māori (Manaia Tuwhare-Hoani, Terina Wichman-Evans, Arihia Hall and Matariki Bennett) who use spoken word as a platform to bring attention to important topics and issues in Aotearoa, especially those that affect Māori. They also weave waiata and te reo Māori through their pieces as their work is strongly driven by their love for their own whakapapa and culture. Ngā Hinepūkōrero earned first place at WORD – The Front Line Slam and the Trans-Tasman Poetry Slam in 2018, and they were semi-finalists at Brave New Voices international youth slam in the US in 2019. In 2020 they received the Ngā Manu Pīrere award for emerging Māori artists at Te Waka Toi Awards.

TŌKU REO

Te reo Māori is the native language of our country
Passed down from generation to generation
Over a single century it almost vanished from a law that suppressed the sound of it in schools
Kids were bruised by their teachers' knuckles for speaking it on the playground
This was their way of delivering us from our wayward state
They viewed our language as the head of a snake
Deemed useless because it wasn't written on paper
It wasn't long until we were forced to speak

In silence

Our kaumatua – **NO. Grandparents'** – lives were stained in blues and purples
English fingers slithering around their necks
Subdued until their sentences were laced with shame
Choking on blood and pride
I can hear their screams
I've never heard them speak

Nowadays being fluent in te reo Māori is a privilege
I've been told how lucky I am to have it as my first language
To speak patterns into the air
Over time it has lost its ability to fly

Language separated from tongue
Like root from tree
So we tuck harakeke – **NO. Flax** – into our cheeks
Stick the fibres between our teeth
Let them knit together in our breath
For if I stay silent my tūpuna – **NO. Ancestors** – will find a way to pry my jaws open
They will weave kete to catch my tears

My grandmother couldn't speak
She was beaten till her jaw was broken
Used the pieces to raise our family
I speak teachings of broken bones
Because no one else in my family could
So tell us to be quiet
And we'll breathe life into ancestors we haven't met
Tell stories of a past submerged in bleach
Legacy lives on in our voices
You can't take them away from us

I hate forgetting
Had to teach myself the prayers – **NO. Karakia** – my parents didn't learn
Had to over-pronounce my words
So the condensed history within each syllable is heard
We learnt not to forget
But to hide
In our whispers
Keeping our culture alive in the bottom of our lungs
We drowned our reo in the depths of our stomachs
Stitched it into our clothes

So tell us to be quiet
And know that we won't
This is our language
We are reclaiming it
We will speak it
For every person that was beaten into silence
We will speak it
For every person that was never taught

We will speak it

We will speak it

We will speak it

Māku tēnei reo e kawe
Mā tōku arero ngā kupu a ōku tūpuna e whakatinana
Kia maumaharatia ai tō rātou nei mataora
Kia kore rātou e koroheketia
Ko wai koe ki te whānako i te poutāwha o ō mātou nei tūpuna?
Patu a kiri
Rere a toto

Anei rā ō mokopuna e tahu ana te ahi

Hei te pō
Hei te ao
Anei rā ngā whenua i mōrehurehu i ōku tūpuna
Ki ngā kino o te Pākehā
Tēnei tōku reo
E haruru ana
I te whenua

IN PRAISE OF IDEOLOGY
spoken word & acoustic sets
Wed 16th July
Wine Cellar
8pm $5 feeds the artists
Courtney Meredith
Anna-Kaye Forsyth
Samuel Braverman
Renee Liang
Andrew Healey
Ed Mecija with Samylka
poetry makes the mind grow fonder

ACID ON THE MICROPHONE
SLAM CHAMPIONS OF THE POETRY WORLD
Carrie Rudzinski and Ken Arkind
alive, righteous and loud
WEDNESDAY JULY 21
Yazza Cafe • 7pm • $10
THURSDAY JULY 22
The Mussel Inn • 7.30pm • Door Sales $10

NEW ZEALAND
POETRY SLAM
NATIONAL FINAL
SATURDAY
NOV 3 2018
HAEATA COMMUNITY CAMPUS AUDITORIUM
240 BREEZES RD, ARANUI, CHCH
EASILY ACCESSIBLE BY BUS.

INTER HIGH SCHOOL POETRY SLAM
Word
THE FRONT LINE
AUCKLAND NEW ZEALAND
2023

MONTANA POETRY SLAM
SAT JULY 28
SLAMMISTRESS RENEE INVITES YOU TO A POETIC TOURNAMENT @ THE LONDON BAR
FEATURING: SPECIAL GUESTS THE LITERATTI
CELEBRITY JUDGES
OVER $400 IN PRIZES
8 PM START
DOOR SALES ONLY $10/$5
Poetry Slam
RULES: 3 MINS MAX PER POEM/ORIGINAL WORK ONLY/ALL CONTESTANTS SELECTED BY AUDITION
TO REGISTER TO COMPETE, CONTACT SLAMMISTRESS RENEE DOCRNZ@GMAIL.COM
SUPPORTED BY MONTANA WINES LTD AND BOOKSELLERS NZ FOR MONTANA POETRY DAY 2007

NGAIO
TKAY
LIV

BASEMENT THEATRE
HOW WE SURVIVE
29 Oct —
2 Nov
Auckland CBD

ANAHERA PRESS
95 bFM
PRESENTS
TICKETS FROM:
1-NIGHT.CO.NZ
REAL GROOVY
CONCH
BEATMERCHANTS
RHYME SUMMIT
AOTEAROA
20/10/2011
7PM
@STUDIO
340 K'RD
FEATURING...
KING KAPISI - KAPA HAKA - SOUL STATION - EASY - MC H-ONE - DUB TERMINATOR + MC MANA - HOLLIE SMITH
ERMEHN - GLENN COLQUHOUN - K-ONE - ROBERT SULLIVAN - QUEEN SHIRL'E - TYSON TYLER - KARLO MILA
WORDPERFECT - SELINA TUSITALA MARSH - PENNY ASHTON - BILLE-FLUID - DARENKAMALI - RUA APERAHAMA - RESIN
JAY ROACHER - JAI MACDONALD - KAY POETA - JINETERO MC - BEN BROWN - GUS SIMONOVIC - CRONIK RE
CHRISTIAN JENSEN - JAHRED LION - PHD - DLAR - BRIGHT SPARKS - BIG SMYLE - BELLA SHANTI - NOWROZE NAYAR
MICHAEL RUDD - MATTHEW HARVEY - TYSON SMITH - THE FEELSTYLE - EMMA HAND - ZANE SCARBOROUGH
PAKKZ THE GENERAL - PROJECTILE - BELLA MAFIA - GRACE TAYLOR - STUNTMAN - SPEARMAN - RAZOR CHEST
SOMETHING DIFFERENT - KIRI PIAHANA-WONG - SIMONE KAHO - FLUENT - UPTOWN SWUITE - BOXX - MC SILVA
LAPSE - IRON WILL - SOLOMONIX - J-KUPA - RADU KID - LEIANA ROBERTSON - CARRIE RUDZINSKI - DOUG POOLE - DENI KAHN
HOSTED BY AMANDA ASHTON (Maori Television)
CENTRAL
rockstar
STUDIO

Stand Up Poetry
North
All Ages Open Mic
7.7.21
STEVIE
DAVIS-TANA

INTER HIGH SCHOOL POETRY SLAM
Word
THE FRONT LINE
AUCKLAND NEW ZEALAND
2021

WRAP YOURSELF IN RIGHTEOUSNESS AND PREPARE FOR A HURRICANE OF WORDS
THE
SLAM
POETRY
SHOW
CARRIE RUDZINSKI
KEN ARKIND
& MARK RAFFILLS
FRIDAY 10 JUNE-7.00 PM
OAMARU OPERA HOUSE
TICKETING INFO: ADULTS: $20; SENIORS: $15; CHILD (18 AND UNDER): $10; (+ SERVICE FEES)
BOOK: OAMARU OPERA HOUSE AND WWW.TICKETDIRECT.CO.NZ

JAFA Poetry
Slam presents
Chants of The
Islands feat.
Terisa
Siagatonu
Special performances by
Grace Taylor
Zech Soakai
Jai Selkirk
Fili Fepulea'i
Friday April 12th
7pm doors / 7:30pm start
$5 students / $10 general
Cityside @ 8 Mount Eden Road
All ages venue.
newzealandpoetryslam@gmail.com

WRITERS FESTIVA
BULA
FIJI

Acknowledgements

We acknowledge the talent, generosity and warmth of the performance-poetry, spoken-word and slam-poetry communities of Aotearoa and beyond. Thank you to those who came before us, who forged the paths we now tread, who made space for our creativity and who shaped our voices.

Thank you to Creative New Zealand and Auckland University Press for believing in this book and supporting its creation. Thank you to our incredible administrator Sarah Dell Enticott, without whom this project would not have been possible. Special thanks to current New Zealand Poet Laureate Chris Tse for his introduction to this collection and to the organisations and individuals who contributed photographs of and posters from our communities.

We would like to credit the many photographers and events whose work is included in this collection: Andi Crown, Andrew Browne, Ankita Singh, Chris Tse, Isoa Kavakimotu, Jocelyn Janon, Markus Ravik, Peniel Fa'amausili, Raymond Sagapolutele, Rebecca Shaw, Going West Writers Festival's Poetry Grand Slam, and Auckland Theatre Company's *My Own Darling*.